EXPERT SYSTEMS IN EDUCATION AND TRAINING

EXPERT SYSTEMS IN EDUCATION AND TRAINING

THOMAS D. McFARLAND & REESE PARKER
LEWIS-CLARK STATE COLLEGE

EDUCATIONAL TECHNOLOGY PUBLICATIONS
ENGLEWOOD CLIFFS, NEW JERSEY 07632

Library of Congress Cataloging-in-the-Publication Data

McFarland, Thomas D.
    Expert systems in education and training / Thomas D. McFarland, O. Reese Parker.
        p.   cm.
    Includes bibliographical references.
    ISBN 0-87778-210-5
    1. Artificial intelligence—Educational applications. 2. Expert systems (Computer science) 3. Computer-assisted instruction.
I. Parker, O. Reese. II. Title.
LB1028.43.M368 1990
371.3'34—dc20
                                                                                89-38713
                                                                                CIP

Printed in the United States of America.

Library of Congress Catalog Card Number:
89-38713.

International Standard Book Number:
0-87778-210-5.

First Printing: January, 1990.

PREFACE

This book is about expert systems and the processes used in their development. Since the concepts and techniques of expert systems development evolve from research in artificial intelligence (AI), a discussion of expert systems necessarily involves the exploration of human and machine intelligence. An understanding of how intelligence works leads toward the solution of many problems in education and training. AI research and development offers intriguing possibilities—but these are possibilities that must be critically evaluated. Controversy currently surrounds the appropriateness of AI applications in education and training. If we are to understand this controversy and judge AI, then we must be knowledgeable about AI issues and concepts. A current question for AI research is "Can computers work smart?" This is a new and complex question for those unfamiliar with AI research and expert systems development. Working smart requires the computer to use knowledge and expertise to guide and inform its education and training efforts.

In recent years, researchers in AI and cognitive science have explored questions related to transferring knowledge and expertise which are of continuing interest to educators and trainers. Research and best practices contribute to a significant body of knowledge and expertise which must to be used to improve education and training. Unfortunately, this knowledge is either stored passively in written materials or in the brains of human experts. If the expert systems development process can increase access to this knowledge and expertise, then improved education and training will result. AI researchers and knowledge engineers acquire and represent knowledge and expertise in accessible knowledge bases. The development of expert systems and intelligent computer-assisted instruction (ICAI) systems permits the transfer of expertise from these knowledge bases to individuals who seek knowledge and information through computer-based consulting and teaching.

The purpose of this book is to provide knowledge and information which will assist educators and training specialists in their evaluation of the field of AI and its possible contribution to their work. Expert systems and ICAI systems are described and illustrated. Information is given to help educators and trainers determine whether expert systems development processes and tools will be helpful in solving educational or training problems specific to their interests. The research, best practices, and opinions of authorities in AI and instruction will be explored. In addition, this book serves as a reference and as a resource for the continued evaluation of AI and expert systems by educators and trainers.

This book is written to accomplish three goals:

1. To discuss the feasibility, utility, and future possibilities of expert systems and intelligent computer-assisted instruction (ICAI) for educators and trainers.

2. To describe the conceptual structures—superordinate, coordinate and subordinate—of AI and expert systems development using terminology and examples which should be interesting and relevant to educators and trainers.

3. To explore the concepts of intelligence and problem solving and their relationship to the transfer of expertise, consulting, and teaching.

The format of this book is designed to accomplish these goals. Each chapter begins with a visual-spatial *Knowledge Map* and brief statement of purpose. Then, an . . . *in the Future* segment shares selected opinions of leaders in AI and the educational technology field about plausible developments in those topics represented in the *Knowledge Map*. The narrative sections of the book describe and illustrate the concepts and techniques of AI and expert systems development through text, tables, and figures. *Boxes* provide supplementary information and examples which may be read independently of the narrative. Critical terms are italicized and carefully defined. A *Chapter Summary* of key points is provided at the end of each chapter. A *Directions* section for each chapter discusses ideas and implications that we perceive to be of special importance to education and training. A judgment *Scorecard* precedes each *Directions* section to allow trainers and educators to record their opinions about the feasibility, effectiveness, enhancing capabilities, and future potential of AI research and development efforts. *Topical References* list primary sources of information at the end of each chapter and a complete listing of all sources of information are provided in the *References* at the end of the book.

This book describes the exploration of AI and expert systems development, and focuses upon the specialized needs and interests of educators and trainers, while assuming that the reader is familiar with the basic concepts and processes of education and training. Therefore, the definitions and examples are drawn from those fields and capitalize upon the identified audiences' existing expertise. Since AI is a new, adolescent field, many of the concepts and processes are poorly defined and described in the AI literature. We have attempted to clarify core concepts and associated processes by searching carefully through the books and articles listed as references. When possible or appropriate, we have paraphrased or quoted definitions from *The Handbook of Artificial Intelligence, The Encyclopedia of Artificial Intelligence*, and the *Dictionary of Artificial Intelligence and Robotics*. We reference definitions and major ideas so that readers may seek out the original source for further information or clarification.

We are optimistic about the increasing use of computer technologies in education and training. Computers are generally accepted as interactive teaching and information tools which can increase work productivity in limited areas. We identify problems which innovative computer technologies can solve and problems where a technological solution may be inappropriate. Although innovative computer technologies from AI are new and unproven, we feel that these new technologies are worthy of respectful study by educators and trainers.

We would like to especially thank our wives, Mary McFarland and Kit Parker, and for their support and assistance during the long process of writing this book. We greatly appreciate the contributions of our colleagues at Lewis Clark State College. In addition, we would like to thank Alan Hofmeister and Stephen Ragan for taking the time to review an early draft of the book.

TABLE OF CONTENTS

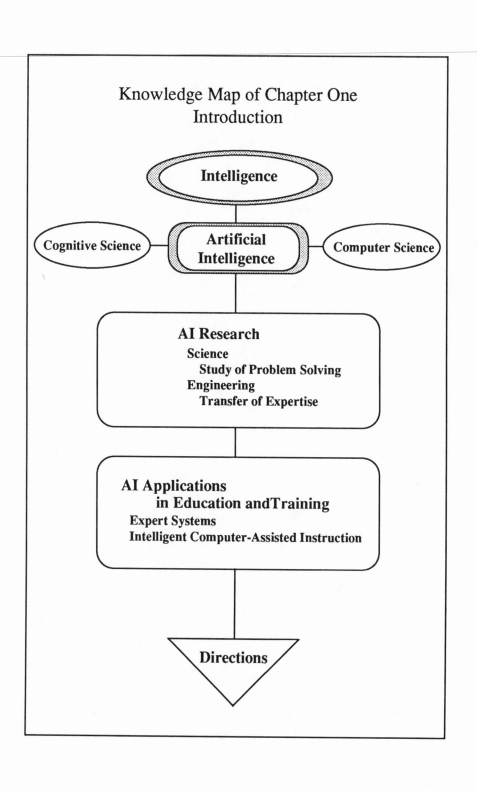

Knowledge Map of Chapter One
Introduction

Intelligence

Cognitive Science — Artificial Intelligence — Computer Science

AI Research
Science
Study of Problem Solving
Engineering
Transfer of Expertise

AI Applications
in Education andTraining
Expert Systems
Intelligent Computer-Assisted Instruction

Directions

1 INTRODUCTION

This chapter overviews the potential of studying human and artificial intelligence. Artificial intelligence (AI) is a field of scientific and engineering research which will lead to the solution of specific problems in education and training. The relationship between AI, cognitive science, and computer science is described. The study of problem solving and transfer of expertise are introduced as major areas of AI research. Expert systems and intelligent computer-assisted instruction (ICAI) are described as AI applications which provide powerful computer-based tools for consulting and teaching.

INTELLIGENT MACHINES IN THE FUTURE

Many science fiction and non-fiction writers describe the potential influence of intelligent machines on life in the 21st century. Imagine the changes that intelligent machines might have on education and training. For example, John Sculley (1987), the Chairman of Apple Computer, describes the "knowledge navigator":

> . . . a discoverer of worlds, a tool as galvanizing as the printing press. Individuals could use it to drive through libraries, museums, databases, or institutional archives. This tool wouldn't just take you to the doorstep of these great resources as sophisticated computers do now, it would invite you deep inside its secrets, interpreting and explaining—converting vast quantities of information into personalized and understandable knowledge. (p. 403)

With your own knowledge navigator, you could explore the "super-highway of knowledge," using the intelligence of your knowledge navigator and its insight into your learning, interests, and needs; you

3

could be guided through the exponentially increasing world of information and knowledge. The knowledge navigator facilitates adaptive teaching and personalized learning. It will become an articulate expert, an intelligent tutor, and a stimulating learning environment.

AI research and development contributes to the feasibility of knowledge navigators in your future. Sculley (1987) describes the pivotal role of AI in the development of the knowledge navigator:

> Artificial intelligence will play an important role in the Knowledge Navigator. Inside the soul of the computer will be intelligent software "agents." Over time, they will become smart enough to learn that you like certain types of information presented in certain ways. The agent will learn along with you and work invisibly, turning information into useful knowledge for you. (p. 408)

The description of knowledge navigators and intelligent software "agents" which contribute to learning are commonplace to educators and trainers. What is unclear is if, when, or how these intelligent problem solvers will impact learning and teaching. Educators and trainers want to understand concepts and processes from AI and other disciplines that will change the real world and our day-to-day lives. For example, Renate Lippert (1989) indicates that:

> Artificial Intelligence (AI) is fast becoming a productive field of inquiry for educational researchers as numerous new conferences and new journals linking AI and education attest to. . . expert systems not only hold great potential for education, but will have a larger impact on education and training than our traditional models of computer-based instruction. (p. 11)

These computer-based tools for consulting and teaching must not only provide promises, but also must meet the evaluative criteria required of other education and training products. In spite of the promise of innovative AI technologies, educators and trainers have seen little impact on their daily lives. Some are becoming cynical about whether intelligent machines are likely to impact education and training settings in the future.

INTELLIGENCE

Informal observations show that individuals differ in their intellectual abilities, and that humans differ from machines. The scientific study of intelligence attempts to describe and explain the mysteries of these differences and the structures and processes of these abilities. Intelligence is an intriguing concept in theory-building and research. As a human characteristic and a potential characteristic of machines, intelligence is a concept which captures the imaginations of philosophers, scientists, and laypersons alike. Numerous books and articles have been written on the topic of intelligence. Many "theories of intelligence" exist. Most of these theories propose to have implications for describing, explaining, predicting, and intervening in human behavior. Few, if any, of these theories have established a level of detail necessary for the construction of machine intelligence.

To be productive, individuals and machines must work hard, work long, but most of all—work smart (Bunderson & Inouye, 1987). Working smart requires an understanding of intelligent behaviors. This practical concern with intelligent behaviors motivates much of the research concerned with it. As noted by Conger (1957):

> ... intelligence is not a thing in any tangible sense. We cannot see it, touch it, or hear it. It is purely a hypothetical construct, a science fiction, like the concept of force in physics. We invent it because it helps us to explain and predict behavior. (p. 15)

The hypothetical construct that intelligence is what intelligence tests measure is used most frequently to predict and intervene. For example, the intelligence test scores of mentally retarded individuals are used to predict the likelihood of their school failure and to intervene with an individualized special education program. The basis for these predictions and interventions is the individual's performance on a standardized intelligence test which samples a range of behaviors considered to be "intelligent" by most people. Although the measurement-oriented approach to intelligence is useful for some purposes of psychology, education, and training; it has limited impact on an understanding of the processes required for intelligent behavior.

Disciplines such as philosophy, psychology, linguistics, anthropology, and neuroscience offer varied approaches to the study of the processes of intelligence. Interdisciplinary researchers seeking to understand the processes of intelligence must explore questions of common interest such as: What are the similarities and differences between the processing of information by humans and machines? What problem solving processes do humans and machines use to act intelligently? The process-oriented approaches to intelligence that are of primary interest to AI are called "information processing."

Intelligence as Information Processing

The *information processing* approach examines not only input and output, but also explores memory and internal processing of information. These studies of cognitive functioning explore sensory processing, coding strategies, and short-, intermediate- and long-term memory. Experiments with human subjects attempt to determine how they receive, store, and retrieve different kinds of information (Hunt, Lunneborg, & Lewis, 1975). This approach to intelligence enables comparisons of the processing of information by humans and by machines.

The information processing approach assumes a mechanistic model of intelligence. That is, it makes the assumption that humans are like machines or computers, and that the processing of information in the human can be described and explained as if the human were a machine. The analogy of a computer allows for a simplified information handling machine—less complex than the brain and central nervous system. This simplification provides the possibility for clearer descriptions and explanations. Obviously, many critics of the information processing approach attack these mechanistic assumptions both in terms of their usefulness and implications for prediction and intervention.

From the founding of AI, the information processing approach has been an assumed model for description, explanation, prediction, and intervention. AI founders, Alan Newell and Herbert Simon, note this relationship:

...the programmed computer and human problem solver are both species belonging to the genus "Information Processing System." (Newell & Simon--Quoted in Weizenbaum, 1976)

Intelligence is an "amalgam of many information-processing and information-representation abilities" according to AI assumptions (Winston & Brady, 1987). Nilsson (1980) emphasizes the relationship of AI research and information-processing theory:

> AI has also embraced the larger scientific goal of constructing an information-processing theory of intelligence. If such a science of intelligence could be developed, it would guide the design of intelligent machines as well as explicate intelligent behavior as it occurs in other animals. (p. 2)

Descriptions and explanations of how intelligence works require an analysis of the components and tasks in the processing of information. Predictions and intervention in AI are based on results of research related to each component. Interventions assert ways to improve the functioning of components such as long-term memory or ways to teach formal reasoning abilities.

Research and development using the information processing approach is not limited to the concept of intelligence, but extends to the concepts of learning and instruction. For example, Gagne (1985) indicates the influence of information processing approaches on education and training:

> The information processing model of learning has important implications for an understanding of instruction. The stimulating conditions that are brought to bear on the learners are not viewed simply as stimuli to which they react. Instead, these external stimuli may be conceived as initiating, maintaining, or otherwise *supporting* several different kinds of ongoing internal processes involved in learning, remembering, and performing. (p. 14)

The interdisciplinary study of information processing by educators and trainers will result in a better understanding of how human and machine intelligence works and how symbolic processing contributes to intelligence and learning.

Intelligence as Symbolic Processing

Knowledge and information are represented as symbols in a computer program. *Symbolic processing* emphasizes the importance of symbols in information processing. Symbols may represent words, concepts, objects, ideas, or procedures. Symbolic processing is significantly different from numeric processing which focuses on numbers and data. The computer is capable of inputting or reading symbols, outputting or writing symbols, storing, copying, and comparing symbols. A fundamental hypothesis of AI is that these symbol manipulating capabilities are those required to exhibit "intelligence" in both humans and machines (Fischler & Firschein, 1987).

AI is a field of research which seeks to solve the symbolic types of problems that experts presently can better solve. When computers were first developed, little distinction was made between intelligent or symbolic processing and unintelligent or numerical computer programs (Carrico, Girard, & Jones, 1989). Basic machine capabilities such as performing calculations were viewed as intelligent tasks. Solving a simple addition problem was considered machine "thinking" and an indication of intelligence. Over a 30 year period, views on what an intelligent program is have changed. Programs must now solve real world problems of much greater complexity to be considered "intelligent."

Intelligence as Problem Solving Processes

Intelligence may be defined as "competency in problem solving," which is a type of general information and symbolic processing (Tennyson &Park, 1984). The study of human and machine intelligence leads to a clarification of how humans and computers solve specific problems. The complexity of the concept *intelligence* has resulted in the necessity of an operational definition. This definition narrows the construct of intelligence to a focus on problem solving processes. Gevarter (1985) indicates that:

> One way of viewing intelligent behavior is as a problem solver. Many AI tasks can naturally be viewed this way, and most AI programs draw much of their strength from their problem solving components. (p. 15)

This ability to solve novel problems by successful behaviors is the problem-solving aspect of the concept "intelligence." Dede (1986) describes the focus of AI as:

> ... expert problem solving in complex, unstructured environments with multiple obstacles and no universal solution algorithm. (p. 330)

The AI method is to build computer programs that simulate and demonstrate "intelligent" behaviors when solving ill-defined problems. These problem solving processes are those without *algorithmic* or a step by step solutions. Gevarter (1985) indicates that:

> The computer programs with which AI is concerned are primarily symbolic processes involving complexity, uncertainty, and ambiguity. These processes are usually those for which algorithmic solutions do not exist and search is required. Thus AI deals with the types of problem solving and decision making that human beings continually face in dealing with the world. (p. 3)

If AI researchers and developers are able to construct an artificial model which functions "intelligently" and solves complex problems, then this method has both theoretical and practical value for education and training.

As computer scientists enabled computers to accomplish many numerical and data processing tasks better than humans, tasks which were once thought to require intelligence became algorithmic, easily understood, replicable, step-by-step procedures. Easily programmed tasks, then, would not be defined as intelligent machine behaviors. Tasks which people are able to perform, while machines are not, become the challenge for AI research. This changing definition of machine intelligence has resulted in a lack of consensus on clear distinctions between intelligent and non-intelligent behavior. This confusion also results in a lack of consensus regarding the characteristics of an "intelligent" computer program and the content of intelligence. Box 1.1 briefly describes the history of changes as AI emerged as a field of inquiry.

Box 1.1

A Brief History of Artificial Intelligence

The study of intelligence has been of concern for centuries, and the idea of mechanizing intelligence predates the idea of the digital computer. Prior to the emergence of the label "Artificial Intelligence," scientists such as Norbert Wiener studied cybernetics, the field involving relationships of animal and machine learning. The first digital computer—the ENIAC—created a high interest in "thinking" machines during World War II. Alan Turing, a British computer scientist, argued that the computer should be designed for symbolic processing with logical operators such as "and" and "or." However, American computer designers prevailed and high speed calculating operations were chosen with numeric operators such as "+" and "-" for "number crunching" in mathematics and science.

The Dartmouth conference of ten mathematics and logic researchers is frequently cited as the beginning of the present field of AI. The planner of the conference, John McCarthy, coined the term "Artificial Intelligence" in the funding proposal. John McCarthy not only provided the name for AI, but also provided the programming language for AI research—LISP. He developed LISP (short for List Processing) in the later 1950's and LISP remains the primary language of AI development. McCarthy founded AI laboratories at Massachusetts Institute of Technology (MIT) and Stanford University. Three other conference attendees have become well-known AI leaders. Allen Newell and Herbert Simon, the developers of an AI program called the General Problem Solver, began and currently work at the AI laboratory at Carnegie-Mellon. Marvin Minsky directed the AI laboratory at MIT and currently is involved in the Media Lab. Many AI scientists have been trained by one of these four individuals. These AI laboratories continue as centers of AI research and development.

ARTIFICIAL INTELLIGENCE

The terms "artificial" and "intelligence" are plainly central concepts of AI. These concepts are not easily defined or described. The concept "artificial" may be used in differing ways. For example, "artificial" light is a useful source for illumination that is similar to natural light, but "artificial" flowers (although potentially useful) are only related to natural flowers in appearance (Sokolowski, 1988). Will the meaning of "artificial" in AI denote both usefulness and reality? Wenger (1987) defines AI as:

> ...the study of principles of computational intelligence as manifested in man-made systems. (p. 8)

Thus, AI may be operationally defined as studying computing machines and the concept of intelligence. Winston (1984) defines AI simply as "the study of ideas that enable the computer to be intelligent." These definitions imply that the terms artificial and computing systems are synonymous, but fail to clarify the meaning of "intelligence."

If "intelligence" is operationally defined as "competence in problem solving," then this definition leads to an emphasis on problem-solving behaviors as demonstrated by either humans or computing machines. AI programs exhibit behavior which is normally identified with human intelligence, but not traditionally identified with computers. For example, humans demonstrate intelligent behavior when they consult one another or make effective decisions. If computers can be programmed to provide effective consultation and decision-making related to specific tasks such as medical diagnosis or to consult with human beings, then their behavior may be defined as "intelligent." An "intelligent" behavior would be demonstrated by the ability to solve novel problems. AI then becomes the process of finding or constructing solutions to problems through the use and study of computing systems.

Initially, AI research explored problem-solving processes of search in structured, puzzle-like tasks. Although AI problem solving processes continue to be the major interest of some researchers, expert systems and knowledge representations are presently the most active area of practical problem solving. AI is emerging as a science and field of inquiry into problem solving processes from the research and development laboratories.   However, applications of AI problem solving processes are only beginning to enter the marketplace.

Artificial intelligence has complex connotations as well as an ill-defined denotation. The term "artificial intelligence" frequently causes controversy and expectations due to the connotations of machine intelligence and expectations that computers may outperform humans in all areas of problem solving and decision making. In recent years, the term "Artificial Intelligence" has developed a positive connotation for practitioners in medicine, science, business, and industry due to the commercial success of expert systems in solving problems in well-defined areas of expertise such as medical diagnosis, chemical analysis, mineral exploration, and equipment repair. One approach to definition is to avoid the multifaceted concepts and connotations and to focus on a description of AI as an interdisciplinary field of research and development in the realm of problem solving.

An Interdisciplinary Field

Artificial intelligence (AI) is an interdisciplinary field of research, application, and instruction which attempts to have computers perform tasks that, if performed by human beings, would be considered intelligent (Simon, 1987). A description of the field of AI and the related fields of cognitive and computer science is needed to clarify the concepts, and explain the importance of continuing efforts to define the field of AI. Many fields contribute to AI research and development.   Figures 1.1 and 1.2 show the interrelationships between AI and cognitive science, and AI and computer science. AI is an interdisciplinary field which is influenced by two new sciences—computer science and cognitive science. AI is a vanguard field of computer science and cognitive science with significant potential for changing each of these sciences.

FIGURE 1.1 Relationship of AI and Cognitive Science

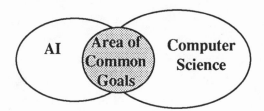

FIGURE 1.2 Relationship of AI and Computer Science

AI and Cognitive Science

Cognitive science investigates the detailed workings of intelligence and problem solving. Cognitive science has been defined as "the study of the principles by which intelligent entities interact with their environments" (Pylyshyn, 1987). The comparative study of intelligent entities includes both humans and machines. Cognitive scientists use these principles to develop workable theories of human intelligence. Mishkoff (1985) indicates:

> As cognitive scientists determine the processes that produce human intelligence in a given situation, these processes may be programmed into a computer in an attempt to simulate that behavior. This AI technique is called modeling or simulation. In effect you are creating a model of intelligent human behavior to try to simulate that behavior on a computer to determine if the computer will exhibit the same intelligent behavior as a human. (p. 1)

Cognitive science is an analytic and rational approach to exploring the symbolic representation, information processing, and computational capabilities of human intelligence as well as the structural and functional aspects of the brain. The nature and representation of knowledge are major concerns of cognitive science research.

Cognitive science is a diverse, interdisciplinary field of study with boundaries which still require definition. Cognitive science research involves contributions from one or more of the following disciplines: psychology, philosophy, linguistics, neuroscience, anthropology, and AI. Box 1.2 describes the confusing overlap between cognitive science and cognitive psychology. Although psychologists, philosophers, and linguists have studied intelligence and cognition for hundreds of years, recent interest in the computer as a model of cognitive processes has resulted in the emergence of this new field. While the study of intelligence and cognition is not new, recent organizations and writings have formed this interdisciplinary field of research. The first meeting of the Cognitive Science Society was held in 1979. A journal, *Cognitive Science,* had been published two years earlier. In recent years, journal articles, books, and reports have been written to describe the principles of cognitive science and clarify the scope and limits of the field (Gardner, 1985).

Cognitive science and AI are closely related and may one day merge (Pylyshyn, 1979). The borders between AI and cognitive science are particularly fuzzy and show considerable overlap. AI has been identified as one of the major disciplines of cognitive science. In a simplified analogy, cognitive science studies the architecture of the human mind while computer science studies the architecture of the computer. AI provides the linkage between cognitive science and computer science. Since the detailed processes of intelligent behavior are unknown, AI research has come forth to assist cognitive science in clarifying these processes. Other disciplines of cognitive science contribute theories, research, and valuable ideas to this endeavor, but these theories and ideas have been too vague and incomplete to be stated in computational terms (Clancey, 1987). AI researchers may work in cognitive science or related disciplines. Cognitive science and AI both explore areas such as language, vision, models of human performance, learning, and expertise. Applications of cognitive science include human-machine interface, teaching methods, communication techniques, prostheses for the handicapped, and methodologies for exploring expertise (Pylyshyn, 1984). As shown by these topics, AI has a significant role in promoting cognitive science research and applications. Scientific research and the desire to know will lead to increasingly useful cognitive technologies and applications.

One major goal of AI emerges from the emphasis of cognitive science. Cognitive science pursues the goal of developing models of how intelligence works and how problems are solved. This goal involves the desire to understand the working of the brain and cognitive processing; to understand the principles of intelligent behavior. Insight into the nature of mind can be gained through developing "intelligent" computer programs. Computer programs force precision and provide a test for computational models of cognition. AI may be described as an attempt to build computer programs that can account for human cognition (Winograd & Flores, 1987). AI focuses cognitive science on the problems of removing this vagueness and designing working models of intelligence.

Box 1.2

Cognitive Science and Cognitive Psychology

As indicated by their names, cognitive psychology and cognitive science each share an interest in cognition—the study of thinking. In addition, cognitive science and cognitive psychology have a considerable amount of overlap in areas and methods of research. *Cognitive psychology* is a branch of psychology which focuses on cognition and the processes of problem solving. Cognitive psychology originated with nineteen century psychologists such as William James, and was very influential in the early decades of the twentieth century.

In practice, the distinctions between cognitive science and cognitive psychology are blurred. Generally, cognitive science tends to emphasize computer modeling to a much greater extent than does cognitive psychology. Cognitive modeling is computer simulation of problem solving processes. Although some cognitive psychologists use computers as models in their theory-building, most concentrate on experimental studies of human or animal subjects. Some cognitive psychologists prefer the label "information-processing psychology" as a descriptor for psychologists who emphasize computer modeling. While cognitive scientists go beyond disciplinary boundaries and frequently consider logical and philosophical perspectives, cognitive psychologists focus more on scientific research and inquiry within the boundaries of psychology.

Cognitive psychology and AI will be linked by their purposes, methods, and theories in the future (Pylyshyn, 1987). Both AI researchers and cognitive psychologists are concerned with intelligence and expertise. Computer simulations are being used to test the theories of some cognitive psychologists. AI concepts will assist cognitive psychologists in theory building. If they are to successfully capture knowledge and expertise on a computer, AI researchers must investigate the theories and research findings of cognitive psychologists.

AI and Computer Science

Computer science is a field of study for individuals committed to the design of computer systems, software development, and computational research. It is the study of how computers work and how computer programs should be constructed. Computer scientists investigate the theories and principles that govern the ability to create, store, modify, and manipulate information. Computer science research and development explores topics such as system analysis, program design, coding, data representation, and design of operating systems (Hopper & Mandell, 1984). The emphasis in computer science is on mathematics and computation as a basis for developing machine techniques.

The computer science and mathematics approach to AI is frequently differentiated from the cognitive science and psychological approach. These alternative perspectives are not necessarily antagonistic, but conflicts of perspective and ownership of AI are noted in many books and articles (Pylyshyn, 1987). For example, some computer scientists and AI researchers consider AI to be merely a branch or topic of computer science. The perspective of the AI-computer scientists is that computer programs need not replicate human approaches to problem solving except when this replication is useful. These computer programs do not attempt to imitate or model humans, but instead capitalize on the rapid data processing capabilities of the machine. This perspective allows programs to maximize the superiority of the computer over humans in areas such as memory. The cognitive science perspective, by contrast, views human approaches to problem solving as the appropriate and more powerful cognitive model for AI science. AI as a part of computer science explores the range of tasks in which computers can assist humans.

A major goal of AI shared with computer science is to make computers more useful and applicable across a wider range of human endeavor. These useful computer programs which incorporate AI concepts and techniques are changing the role of computers in our lives (Winston, 1984). AI advances computer science research by enhancing computer programming methods. The innovative applications resulting from AI research complement traditional computer programming. For example, AI languages and techniques are becoming required topics of computer science study. These AI languages and techniques will merge with computer science techniques to become commonplace. The by-products of this AI research and development include object-oriented languages, visual interfaces, windows, pop-up menus, icons, and mouse input devices (Rauch-Hindin, 1988). AI challenges the limits of computer science and technology because AI programs that model intelligence must be "massive and complex" (Winston & Brady, 1987). The problems of AI are difficult and interesting for computer scientists. Research in AI expands computer science by exploring ideas and methodologies of computational intelligence.

AI Research

Areas of AI research are currently divided into two major branches—science and engineering. For example, the annual conference of the American Association of Artificial Intelligence classifies presentations as either of scientific or engineering interest. The concern of AI science with theory building and understanding both human and machine intelligence may be differentiated from product directed concerns of building expert systems. However, AI science and engineering are not independent. Although some conflicts of interest occur, AI science coexists with the AI engineering discipline (Wenger, 1987). The boundaries that define AI science and engineering will gradually shift as AI techniques which emerge from research laboratories become commonly accepted and used in applied settings and product development.

Research relies upon the scientific method to examine the information and to draw conclusions from the findings and facts. AI scientists are primarily concerned with studying problem solving and reasoning in the abstract. Many AI scientists explore problem solving through academic research programs at major universities and laboratories (Harmon & King, 1985). These AI scientists seek general techniques for solving broad classes of problems. Scientific research in AI, like scientific research in general, focuses on hypothesis testing. The contribution of AI science is the exploration of theoretical issues in problem analysis, knowledge representation, reasoning methodologies, and heuristic search strategies. AI techniques such as knowledge representation, reasoning and inference methods, and heuristic search-based problem-solving methods will be clarified and illustrated in Chapter Two.

AI research occurs in numerous areas of computer and cognitive science. The role of research is to seek areas where knowledge is incomplete and to solve problems which need solutions. AI researchers seek to identify relevant knowledge and information related to human and machine problem-solving capabilities. For example, AI scientists study natural language processing, speech recognition, computer vision, robotics, and automatic programming. Box 1.3 describes areas of AI research which attempt to enhance human capabilities.

AI engineering attempts to apply research findings in the development of useful "intelligent" computer programs. AI engineers work with AI scientists to apply symbolic representation and symbolic inference procedures of real-world problems. According to Carrico, Girard, and Jones (1989):

> ... AI can be considered a group of problem-solving techniques or tools
> that emulate human thought to help in increasing knowledge, processing
> productivity, or making decisions. (p. 3)

Applications of AI research are of current commercial interest because of the success of several research projects. The success of expert systems in the commercial marketplace has led to high interest in AI engineering.

Transfer of expertise is a major area of research for both engineers and scientists. Some individuals working toward the transfer of expertise call themselves "knowledge engineers." *Knowledge engineers* use AI concepts and techniques. Knowledge engineers develop expert systems and intelligent computer assisted instruction (ICAI) systems through a systematic process of planning, designing, constructing, and evaluating expert systems. Knowledge engineers focus on capturing and encoding knowledge, reasoning, and expertise in problem solving areas that can be defined, organized, and structured. Knowledge engineering processes assist individuals in analyzing and solving complex problems. Knowledge engineers use AI programming languages and expert systems development tools in the construction of prototypes and in working AI programs. Expert systems development tools may be used in clarifying knowledge and developing products for education and training. Knowledge engineering will complement the research and development area of instructional design. Both processes seek to clarify expertise and to transfer that expertise to novices.

Transfer of expertise from humans to machines and back to other humans is a major goal of AI research and development. A major question pursued by AI scientists and knowledge engineers is "How can problem solving abilities and expertise be organized so that they can be used for consulting and teaching?" Figure 1.3 shows a transfer of expertise model which may be applied in the development of knowledge bases, expert systems, and ICAI systems. As shown, domain expertise is captured in a knowledge base by the knowledge engineer. Then this knowledge base may be used as a source for either consultation through an expert system or teaching through an ICAI system.

AI APPLICATIONS IN EDUCATION AND TRAINING

Two related areas of AI application which merge with research and development in education and training are expert systems and intelligent computer-assisted instruction (ICAI). These applications use concepts and techniques from AI and knowledge engineering to improve consultation and teaching. Research on the transfer of expertise contributes to the development of better expert systems and ICAI systems. Overlap exists between the development of expert systems and ICAI systems in that an expert system may serve as a module for an ICAI system. Some products of AI may be considered as either ICAI systems or expert systems. For example, GUIDON, a classic ICAI program that teaches medical diagnosis began with the development of MYCIN, a diagnostic expert system.

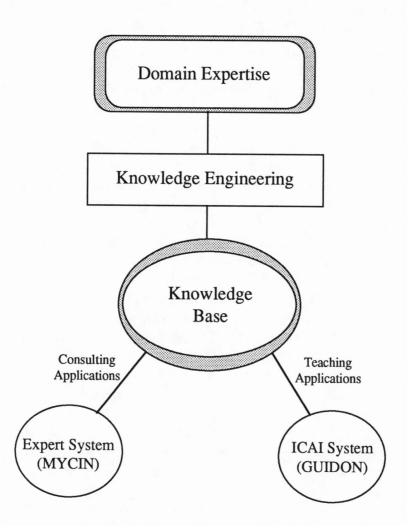

FIGURE 1.3 Transfer of Expertise

Box 1.3

Areas of AI Research and Development

Most areas of AI research emphasize the amplification of human capabilities. Although humans are able to demonstrate amazing capabilities in many areas, machine amplification is needed to compensate for human limitations in some areas of communication, motor, and learning.

One AI research area which complements human capabities in communication is called *natural language processing*. Natural language processing includes both the understanding and generation of natural languages such as English. Natural language processing requires a synthesis of cognitive science research in linguistics and cognition with computer science research in high speed processing of information. Simplifying communication with computers through a natural language interface has been an important area of AI research since the development of computers. For example, SHRDLU is a classic program developed by Winograd (1972) which was capable of understanding and answering questions about its limited world of blocks. Most work in natural language processing focuses on text or typed and displayed information. Complex computer programs are presently able to "read" and interpret books, magazines, and journals.

Speech recognition will additionally enable computers to understand oral communication. The goal of speech recognition is to allow computers to understand spoken language at the level of competence of a human listener. For example, HEARSAY II, a Carnegie-Mellon University project, analyzes communication at several levels using a blackboard workspace to improve speech recognition. Improvements in speech recognition have resulted in commercial systems that have large vocabularies and the capabilities of interpreting flowing speech. *Speech synthesis* programs provide computers with the capabilities of speaking while natural language processing provides them with the capabilities of knowing what to say.

Computational vision focuses on the successful interpretation of two- and three-dimensional images. In computational vision, light waves are transformed by signal processing techniques into digitized images which then must be analyzed and interpreted. Many studies of computer vision were first explored in the simplified context of block worlds with a limited set of three dimensional objects. For example, Waltz (1975) extended previous block world research to include shadows, cracks, and concave edges. Computational vision is an important feature of an intelligent robot.

Robotics research has been augmented by AI research. While non-intelligent robots execute programmed mechanical manipulation, AI techniques seek to provide adaptability and an understanding of the robot's environment. A camera and other sensing devices must be used to provide the information, about the environment, required for intelligent decision-making. Mobile robots and robotic vision are important areas of research with significant potential in defense and industry (Mishoff, 1985).

Machine learning is a major area of AI research which will provide computers with the capabilities of improving their performance. Machine learning has explored several types of learning: rote learning, taking advice, learning from examples, and concept learning. For example, AM is a machine learning program that seeks to discover concepts of set theory and elementary mathematics through a complex search and refinement process after starting with a large body of concepts from finite set theory (Cohen & Feigenbaum, 1982).

Expert systems are computer programs which capture the knowledge of experts in a domain. Expert systems are emerging from the research laboratories, and are now used as practical applications in a variety of settings. However, research on expert systems continues to focus on knowledge representation, machine reasoning, heuristic programming, and interface systems. Obviously, the description of expert systems research is expanded throughout this book.

Expert Systems

Expert systems are computer programs that are capable of consultation, decision support, and job performance assistance based upon their contained expertise in a specific problem solving area. In order for expert systems to offer valid advice or assistance, this expertise must be captured using the concepts and techniques from AI and knowledge engineering. Expert systems are computer programs that are developed to perform difficult problem solving tasks at the same levels as a competent individual. To function at such levels, expert systems require a large body of specific knowledge in a well-defined problem area. The roles of expert systems vary.

> Expert systems are a class of computer programs that can advise, analyze, categorize, communicate, consult, design, diagnose, explain, explore, forecast, form concepts, identify, interpret, justify, learn, manage, monitor, plan, present, retrieve, schedule, test, and tutor (Michaelsen, Michie, & Boulanger, 1985, p. 303)

Barr and Feigenbaum (1982) limit the definition of expert systems by describing the requirements for an effective expert system:

> For an expert system to be truly useful, it should be able to learn what the human expert knows, so that it can perform as well as they do, understand the points of departure among the views of human experts who disagree, keep its knowledge up to date as human experts do (by reading, asking questions, and learning from experience), and present its reasoning to its human users in much the same way that human experts would (justify, clarifying, explaining, and even tutoring). (p. 80)

A less restricted definition of expert systems is offered by Harmon and King (1985) when they define *expert systems* to mean:

> Any computer system developed by a loose collection of techniques associated with AI research. (p. 259)

If accepted, this less demanding definition includes a wider range of computer system products which provide job assistance and decision support under the label "expert systems." These computer-based tools would be useful in transferring knowledge, however, they need not capture the expertise of high-level domain experts or learn from experience.

Expert systems originally referred to expert consultant programs which were developed after intensive efforts to capture the best expertise of practitioners in the specific domain. However, few expert systems presently available offer expert advice. Some merely capture ordinary and useful knowledge which may be valuable only to novices. Only a few expert systems truly offer advice at a level consistent with the best experts in their domain. Recently, some AI researchers and developers have preferred the term "knowledge systems" to expert systems since the commercial and applied efforts have often focused on capturing knowledge which differentiates novices and competent performers. These knowledge systems do not rival human experts in their performance and so may not deserve the commonly used label "expert" (Harmon & King, 1985). These knowledge systems have demonstrated usefulness in many areas of business and industry, but fail to perform at the same high levels as human expertise. However, since the term "expert systems" has gained such popularity, a change to knowledge systems terminology has not appeared except in a few settings. Chapter Four describes and illustrates three types of expert systems—expert consultants, job performance aids, and decision support systems.

Expert systems offer consultation or decision support based upon expertise related to specific tasks. An expert system performs problem solving by engaging the user in a dialogue which parallels the session a person might have with a consultant who has the specific desired expertise. The computer program asks questions that clarify the problem and requests facts and information needed by the expert system to suggest one or more solutions, provide advice, or guide a decision-making process. Many expert systems have the capabilities to explain why the consultant program has asked a question, to show the rules used in the search for a solution, and to assign confidence factors to each solution. The description of a consultation with an expert system is further clarified through a MYCIN example provided in Box 1. 4.

Box 1.4

MYCIN—Expert System

MYCIN is a knowledge-based consultation program which provides expert advice on specific cases in the diagnosis and treatment of specific types of infections. It is appropriate that the MYCIN project is frequently chosen as the prototype example of an expert system by writers of introductory books on AI and expert systems. MYCIN, as the "granddaddy" of expert systems, clearly illustrates the important concepts of an expert system. MYCIN is described in the AI literature by its own book, *The Rule-Based Expert Systems— The MYCIN Experiments of the Stanford Heuristic Programming Project* (Buchanan & Shortliffe, 1984) and in many other books and articles. In addition, the MYCIN project continues today with work by Clancey and his colleagues in the development of knowledge-based tutoring programs such as GUIDON2. GUIDON will serve as the prototype example for intelligent computer-assisted instruction (ICAI) later in this chapter. The MYCIN program is one of the prototypes developed through years of research which has been shown to offer consultation equivalent to the best experts in its knowledge domain of medicine.

MYCIN was developed to demonstrate the potential of capturing expert knowledge in medicine. It was developed to meet the need of physicians in the diagnosis and treatment of infections that involve bacteria in the blood or meningitis. Since these infections can be fatal, the physician frequently must begin treatment without a complete set of laboratory reports. Classification and diagnosis of infections requires high levels of specific expertise. Diagnosis and treatment frequently mandate consultation with specialists. In addition, research indicates that many physicians without adequate expertise who have proceeded with treatment of infections failed to treat the problem with appropriate medications.

MYCIN begins a consultation with the following instructions:

This is a computer program named MYCIN that has been designed to advise you regarding an appropriate choice of infectious disease therapy. It is understood that you have a patient who may have an infection. Please answer the following questions. . . . If you are not certain of your answer, you may modify the response by inserting a certainty factor (a number from 1 to 10) in parentheses after your response. Absolute certainty (10) is assumed for every unmodified answer.

Note that you may also enter *UNK* (for UNKnown) if you do not know the answer to a question, *?* if you wish to see a more precise definition of the question or some examples of recognized responses, *??* if you want to see all recognized responses, the word *RULE* if you would like to see the decision rule which has generated the question being asked, the word *WHY* if you would like to see a more detailed explanation of the question, or the letters *QA* if you would like to interrupt the consultation in order to ask questions regarding the decisions made so far in the consultation.

The following is a sample question and *WHY* explanation taken from a dialogue:

Is Pt538 a burn patient?
***WHY
Why is it important to determine whether Pt538 has been seriously burned?
[4.0] This will aid in determining the organism (other than those seen on cultures or smears) which might be causing the infection.
It has already been established that
[4.1] the infection which requires therapy is meningitis, and
[4.2] organisms were not seen on the stain of this pending CSF culture, and
[4.3] the type of the infection is bacterial
Therefore, if [4.4] Pt538 has been seriously burned
then there is suggestive evidence (.5) that pseudomonas-aeruginosa is one of the organisms (other than those seen on cultures or smears) which might be causing the infection

A complete sample MYCIN consultation may be found in the Appendix of Buchanan and Shortliffe (1984).

Intelligent Computer-Assisted Instruction

Intelligent computer-assisted instruction (ICAI) systems are computer based instructional systems which emphasize intelligent learning environments and intelligent tutoring systems and combine modules of simulation, expertise, teaching, and diagnostic-student modeling. According to Dede (1986):

> Educational devices incorporating artificial intelligence (AI) would 'understand' *what, who* and *how* they were teaching and could therefore tailor content and methods to the needs of an individual learner without being limited to repertoire or prespecified responses (as are conventional computer assisted instruction systems). (p. 329)

ICAI research and development efforts have demonstrated the feasibility of improving computer-based instruction through a range of studies in cognitive science, computer science, and AI. As indicated, cognitive and computer science are two fields which have goals of finding out how intelligence works and designing intelligent programs reflecting their findings. ICAI researchers have developed computer-based instruction tutors and learning environments that demonstrate intelligence in their interactions with students. The cognitive science emphasis of ICAI focuses upon better understanding of cognitive processes in problem solving and transfer of expertise. Computer-based instructional systems which incorporate AI concepts and processes are being explored to determine the potential of "intelligent" tutoring and learning environments in education and training. Like expert systems, ICAI systems are developed to interact knowledgeably with users.

ICAI research and development can be classified into two types—intelligent tutoring systems (ITS) and intelligent learning environments. As previously indicated, some expert systems are capable of explaining their reasoning, and as such have instructional potential. Intelligent tutoring systems (ITS) are an important focus of computer-based instruction. The emphasis on student problem-solving has resulted in intelligent tutoring systems which emphasize "learning-by-doing" (Sleeman & Brown, 1982). Classic ITS prototypes have explored diagnostic tutoring, coaching, and dialogues which can be initiated by the students. AI has explored the impact of computer-based learning environments such as LOGO microworlds, knowledge-based simulations, and other artificial environments on education and training. Intelligent learning environments, as the name indicates, are interactive and reactive environments for creating and experimenting with decisions.

These ICAI research and development efforts propose to significantly transform education and training through simulating problem solving environments, adaptive teaching, the understanding of domain expertise, and the diagnosis of student learning. ICAI is a modular approach to computer-based instruction which seeks to develop separate models of the simulation environment, the expert's problem solving processes, effective teaching strategies, and the student's problem solving efforts. ICAI intends to combine the simulation module, expertise module, teaching module, and student module into an integrated computer-based instructional system. Present research and development focuses on the plan and design of a small number of ICAI prototype programs which emphasize one or more of these modules. This modular approach allows researchers to explore and develop each of the modules separately (Park, Perez, & Seidel, 1987).

The workings of an ICAI system are best described through the GUIDON example shown in Box 1.5 and other examples provided in Chapter Five. GUIDON is a classic ICAI program which clearly illustrates important components and processes of intelligent learning environments and tutoring. The GUIDON project represents a long-term effort to convert MYCIN, an expert system, into an ICAI program. The GUIDON project and the recent work on GUIDON2 are important prototypes in the exploration of the modular approach to the development of an ICAI systems. Chapter Five focuses on the impact of ICAI systems and expert systems on adaptive teaching through the development of simulation, expertise, teaching, and student modules.

Box 1.5

GUIDON—ICAI System

The goals of the GUIDON project were to assess the usefulness of the MYCIN rule-based knowledge for teaching, to explore the additional knowledge required for effective teaching, and to develop a separate rule-based teaching module which operates independently of the MYCIN expertise module. The GUIDON program utilizes the MYCIN expert system as a source or expertise module for teaching. MYCIN rules were not modified for the first version of GUIDON. To accomplish all the goals of the project, a revised version called NEOMYCIN was later developed to work with GUIDON2. NEOMYCIN restructures the expert system MYCIN to separate the explicit diagnostic strategies, used by an expert, from specific medical knowledge related to bacterial infections (Clancey, 1987).

The teaching module was developed with a large set of rules to guide the student's interactions with the program. GUIDON's teaching rules focus upon communicating knowledge which includes when to intervene, and how to select and present relevant information. A case method teaching approach is used by GUIDON. GUIDON selects cases and describes them to the medical student who acts as a diagnostician. The program interrupts the student during suboptimal decisions. A mixed-initiative format allows either the student to ask questions during the case, or for GUIDON to ask questions of the student. Communication with the program requires simple sentences or "help," "details," "justify," and "summary" commands (Wenger, 1987).

The student module uses an overlay on the MYCIN rulebase. GUIDON assesses overall mastery and tries to determine which rules the program believes the student did apply and which rules the program believes the student could apply. Problems encountered in the development of GUIDON have led to a better understanding of diagnosis and to a better understanding of the teaching and consultation process.

The following are instructions taken from sample dialogues between a medical student and GUIDON.

> You are to play the role of consultant for a patient suspected to have an infection. After initial data has been presented, you should request more information about the patient, decide which organisms (if any) require therapy, and prescribe treatment. The tutor will direct you, according to the profile you set. Its behavior can vary from leaving you alone until you are ready to make a diagnosis, to directing your thinking at every step. Feel free to change your profile or request HELP to solve the problem at any time. Use a question mark (?) whenever you want to see the list of options open to you. Remember that the purpose of this session is to present MYCIN's rules of infectious disease diagnosis and, in the second part, the criteria of therapy selection.

After receiving initial case data and developing a session profile on the student, a sample dialogue follows (Student in all capitals):

> What are the organisms that might be causing the infection?
> **NEISSERIA-MENINGITIS
> What facts about this case tell you that Neisseris-meningitis is one of the organisms that be causing the infection?
> (Enter one factor per line.)
> **AGE
> **
>
> None of the factors that you mentioned are appropriate:
> —The age of J. Smith is not evidence for the conclusion that Neisseria-meningitis is one of the organisms that might be causing the infection.
>
> After gaining more information about this case, the age of J. Smith will enable us to conclude that the organisms that might be causing the infection are:
> e. coli (considering whether the infection was acquired when the patient was hospitalized [Rule 545]).

For a complete protocol, see Appendix C in *Knowledge-Based Tutoring—The GUIDON Program* (Clancey, 1987).

CHAPTER SUMMARY

• Intelligence may be operationally defined as competence in problem solving. Interdisciplinary studies of intelligence seek to describe and explain the structure and process of intelligence. The information processing approach focuses on the components and tasks in the processing of information. Symbolic processing emphasizes the importance of symbols such as words, concepts, objects, and ideas in information processing.

• Artificial intelligence is an interdisciplinary field of research, application, and instruction. AI explores the process of constructing solutions to problems through the use and study of computing systems. AI is a changing concept which has complex connotations and ill-defined denotations.

• Cognitive science and AI share the goal of understanding how problems are solved and how intelligence may be modeled on a machine. Cognitive science is an interdisciplinary field of study involving contributions from psychology, philosophy, linguistics, neuroscience, anthropology, and AI.

• AI shares the goal of applying those understandings to the development of useful computer programs with computer science. Computer science investigates the principles that govern the ability to create, store, modify, and manipulate information. AI as a part of computer science explores the challenging problems in which computers can assist humans.

• AI research is divided into two major branches—science and engineering. Areas of AI research are machine learning, natural language processing, robotics, and computational vision. AI scientists explore problem solving and research in the abstract. Knowledge engineers use AI concepts and techniques to improve the transfer of expertise.

• Educational and training applications in AI include expert systems and intelligent computer-assisted instruction (ICAI). These application areas are testbeds for demonstrating AI tools and processes. In addition, these AI products will become useful computer-based consultants and adaptive teaching systems.

• Expert systems are computer programs developed to provide consultation and to perform difficult tasks at or beyond levels at which human experts are able to perform. Performance at this level of expertise requires that the expert system have specific knowledge in well-defined problem solving areas. Expert systems make decisions based upon facts, rules and heuristics acquired through a knowledge engineering process. Expert systems are frequently able to explain their reasoning by showing the facts and rules used in their applied decision-making activities.

• Intelligent computer-assisted instruction (ICAI) combines traditional computer-based instruction with innovative approaches which incorporate methods from AI. Two general types of ICAI are intelligent tutoring systems (ITS) and intelligent learning environments. The simulation module, expertise module, student module, and teaching module are components of an ICAI program and the current focal points for ICAI research. Computer-based learning environments which provide artificial worlds (microworlds), empowering tools, and hypermedia applications for education and training, are promising areas for development in the near future. ITS prototypes demonstrate the adaptive teaching capabilities of mixed-initiative dialogue, diagnostic tutors, and coaches.

USING THE SCORECARDS

As educators and trainers examining and evaluating AI research and development for perhaps the first time, it may be useful to keep a "Scorecard" of your judgments. Each chapter of the book explores different topics related to AI and expert systems. After each chapter and at the end of the book, record a descriptor of your reactions to the feasibility, effectiveness, enhancing capacity, and potential usefulness of each topic impacting education and training. Column 1 represents the dimension of simple feasibility—For example, are expert systems feasible? Column two represents the effectiveness dimension—For example, can AI research positively impact the effectiveness of current practices in education and training? The third column addresses the dimension of enhanced capabilities. Will AI applications such as ICAI be likely to enable educators and trainers to add capabilities to their current range and levels of expertise? The final column concerns the dimension of plausible future utility. Is there something sufficiently intriguing going on to invite educators and trainers to follow progress and hold final judgment in abeyance?

Your reactions may be recorded as simple descriptors such as: "Yes," "No," or "Unsure." However, if you have either strong positive or negative reactions, you may wish to write your own descriptors such as: "Impossible," "Inplausible," or "Absolutely."

In addition to the Scorecard, space has been allowed to make brief comments. We will discuss our reactions and opinions in each of the Directions sections following each chapter's Scorecard.

Topics	Question Dimensions			
	Feasibility	Improved Effectiveness	Capacity Enhancing	Future Utility

SCORECARD

Will AI Research and Development Efforts Contribute to Education and Training?

Topics	Feasibility	Improved Effectiveness	Capacity Enhancing	Future Utility
Intelligence				
Artificial Intelligence				
AI–Cognitive Science				
AI–Computer Science				
AI Research				
Expert Systems				
Intelligent Computer-Assisted Instruction				

Comments:

DIRECTIONS

You are a stranger to a strange culture. You look around and what you see is exciting. As you observe, you find the ideas are new, and the activities are interesting. However, your time is valuable and you cannot spend a long time in this culture unless it will be of long-term significance. When you return to your own culture, you want to take with you the products and ideas that will be most useful.

Then you begin to experience culture shock. You cannot seem to speak the language clearly and have difficult communicating with the natives. The natives of this culture appear to have different values. You have difficulty evaluating their ideas and judging the usefulness of the products around you. Your cultural values are confused by your encounters. You begin to hear things about your own culture that challenge your own assumptions. You become confused and do not know what is true. You start to question your own values.

Some individuals experience cultural excitement and some culture shock when they first encounter a new field and culture such as AI. Since their understanding is limited, they have difficulty evaluating the new field. At times, this challenge to values and assumptions might be useful and helpful. However, often this confusion leads to giving up on the new field.

Artificial intelligence (AI) is a research and development field which presents many exciting ideas to educators and trainers. However, the differences between the field of AI and that of education and training seem so significant that the educator or trainer may become disoriented in this alien culture. This disorientation may lead to an inability to differentiate the useful from the useless. In addition, the comments from AI leaders and researchers about education and training may challenge deeply held values and assumptions. Since they do not know or understand the educational culture, some of their assessments will be incorrect and naive.

In some cases, their naive statements about education and training may make you angry. We may wonder, why haven't they taken the time to get to know our culture better?

Cultural resistance is a barrier to acceptance of new technologies such as expert systems. Cultural resistance is based upon how different cultural groups understand the goals and terminology of the new technology. For example, AI applications derive from computer science and cognitive science. The goal of finding out how intelligence works is of equal to concern to education, training, cognitive science, and AI. The goal of designing useful and intelligent computer programs is shared by computer science, education, training, and AI. These shared goals lead to the need for interdisciplinary efforts.

Unfortunately, diverse cultures also have diverse goals and values. The AI contextual definition of "a useful computer program" is different from that of education and training. For example, educators and trainers demonstrate usefulness in real-world settings while AI researchers test usefulness in their laboratories. Most educators and trainers will judge AI on the issue of usefulness. Expert systems, ICAI systems, and other AI technologies will be evaluated to a great extent by educators and trainers and their acceptance or rejection will be based upon whether they find these systems to be useful in their specific settings. If AI technologies are to be used in education and training, then these new technologies must be shown to be useful and transferrable from research to applied settings.

Cultural diversity may have positive impact if it leads to better understanding of both your own and other cultures. A successful interdisciplinary effort requires an understanding and synthesis of concepts and processes from many fields of inquiry. This interdisciplinary research and development will lead to many applications in education and training. To overcome cultural resistance and cultural diversity, educators and trainers must gain a better understanding of AI.

Educational settings have acquired the reputation of being resistant to new technologies. Training settings, although somewhat resistant to change, have usually been more successful in transferring useful research and development from new technologies into practice. Educators and trainers must continue to be critical of new technologies which fail to transfer to their settings. Research and best practices in technology transfer show roles, guidelines, and observations that usually result in successful diffusion of new technologies. Pioneers or innovators have a role to play in the adaptation of AI technologies. Pioneers are individuals who adopt technologies quickly. These early innovators learn about a new technology and come up with ideas for implementation in the educational or training organization. Unfortunately, pioneers will not bring new technologies such as expert systems into an organization without support. The pioneer or early innovator must convince an organization's leadership of the usefulness of expert systems if they are to be transferred into education and training.

We are almost certain that the conception of intelligence as problem solving will increase the future utility of this concept. Limiting the connotation and denotation to IQ test-based definitions has additionally limited the uses of that concept. Adopting the frame of reference of intelligence as the capability to solve novel problems represents an AI contribution which will improve the fields of education and training. The widespread use and extention of the concept of intelligence in education and training should improve current effectiveness, lead to capacity enhancing developments in the field, and will have great future utility. It is important that collaborative efforts produce practical applications from this extend concept of intelligence.

Knowledge engineering techniques and focusing upon the transfer of expertise will also contribute to education and training. All educators and trainers seek to move their students toward becoming "experts" as a result of instructional interventions. Yet, few educators or trainers approach the design and implementation of instruction with the specific intent to enable their students or trainees to capture and use expertise. Adopting a transfer of expertise perspective holds the promise of rapid improvements in current practices and enhancing the capacity of education and training. Perhaps most importantly, as more and more domains of expertise are subject to knowledge engineering processes, educators and trainers will have a much clearer picture of the knowledge and skills they are trying to teach to others. Further, knowing the structure of expert operations and decisions in those domains will lend significant insight into controversies regarding content versus process orientations that plague many fields of instructional endeavor in contemporary education and training settings.

Finding out how intelligence works—the shared goal of AI and cognitive science—is seen as an equally important goal for education and training. Given the close relationship between the knowledge engineering processes and systematic processes in education and training, the merger of these systematic processes seems likely in the future. Designing intelligent computer programs—the shared goal of AI and computer science—is judged to be somewhat less likely to produce contributions in education and training until some more distant future date. Computer science, as a field of practice, has criteria and processes which are judged to be most alien to education and training. We predict that intelligent computer programs for education and training are more likely to be produced by practitioners gaining and applying expertise in computer-based instruction than computer scientists producing intelligent tutoring programs with minimal help from educators and trainers. When intelligent programs meet the design demands of education and training environments, there is a high probability that AI-computer scientists may judge them to be unintelligent.

TOPICAL REFERENCES

Intelligence

Fischler, M.A., & Firschein, O. (1987). *Intelligence: The eye, the brain, and the computer.* Reading, MA: Addison-Wesley Publishing.

Sternberg, R.J. (1982). *Handbook of human intelligence.* Cambridge, MA: Cambridge University Press.

Artificial Intelligence

Gevarter, W.B. (1985). *Intelligent machines—An introductory perspective of artificial intelligence and robotics.* Englewood Cliffs, NJ: Prentice-Hall, Inc.

Mishkoff, H.C. (1985). *Understanding artificial intelligence.* Dallas, TX: Texas Instruments.

Cognitive Science

Gardner, H. (1985). *The mind's new science .* New York: Basic Books.

Pylyshyn, Z. (1987). Cognitive science. In S.C. Shapiro (Ed.)*The encyclopedia of artificial intelligence–Vol. I.* New York: John Wiley & Sons.

Computer Science

Hopper, G.M., & Mandell, S.L. (1984). *Understanding computers .* St. Paul, MN: West Publishing.

Shelly, G.B., & Cashman, T.J. (1984). *Computer fundamentals for an information age .* Brea, CA: Anaheim Publishing.

AI Research

Barr, W., & Feigenbaum, E.A. (Eds.) (1982). *The handbook of artificial intelligence–Volume II.* Los Altos, CA: William Kaufmann, Inc.

Cohen, P.R., & Feigenbaum, E.A. (Eds.) (1982). *The handbook of artificial intelligence–Volume III.* Los Altos, CA: William Kaufmann, Inc.

Expert Systems

Carrico, M.A., Girard, J.E., & Jones, J.P. (1989). *Building knowledge systems–Developing and managing rule-based applications.* New York: Intertext Publications–McGraw-Hill.

Hayes-Roth, F., Waterman, D.A., & Lenat, D.B. (1983). *Building expert systems.* Reading, MA: Addison-Wesley Publishing.

Harmon, P., & King, D. (1985). *Expert systems—Artificial intelligence in business.* New York: John Wiley & Sons.

Harmon, P., Maus, R., & Morrissey, W. (1988). *Expert systems tools and applications.* New York: John Wiley & Sons.

Rauch-Hindin, W.B. (1988). *A guide to commercial artificial intelligence.* Englewood Cliffs, NJ: Prentice-Hall, Inc.

Waterman, DA. (1986). *A guide to expert systems.* Reading, MA: Addison-Wesley Publishing.

Intelligent Computer-Assisted Instruction

Clancey, W.J. (1986). From GUIDON to NEOMYCIN and HERACLES in Twenty Short Lessons: ORN Final Report 1979-1985. *AI Magazine, 7* (3), 40-60.

Clancey, W.J. (1987). *Knowledge-Based Tutoring—The GUIDON program.* Cambridge, MA: The MIT Press.

Dede, C. (1986). A review and synthesis of recent research in Intelligent Computer-Assisted Instruction. *Journal of Man-Machine Studies, 24,* 329-353.

Kearsley, G. (Ed.) (1987). *Artificial intelligence and instruction— Applications and methods.* Reading, MA: Addison-Wesley Publishing.

Sleeman, D., & Brown, J.S. (Eds.) (1982). *Intelligent tutoring systems.* London: Academic Press.

Wenger, E. (1987). *Artificial intelligence and tutoring systems— Computational and cognitive approaches to the communication of knowledge.* Los Altos, CA: Morgan Kaufmann Publishers.

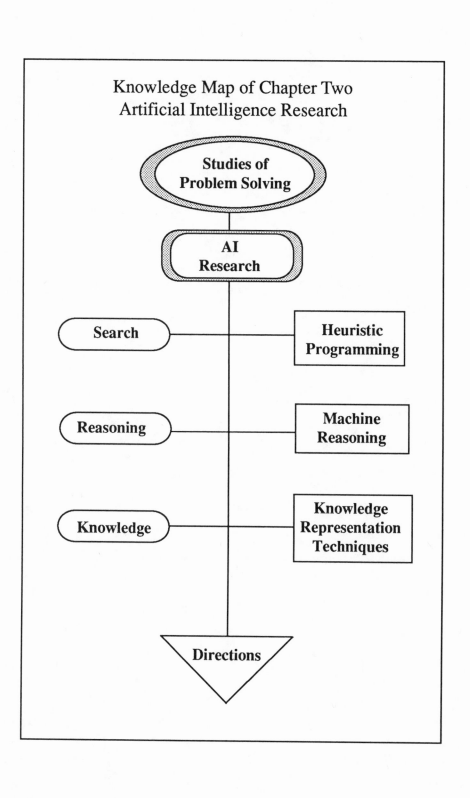

Knowledge Map of Chapter Two
Artificial Intelligence Research

Studies of
Problem Solving

AI
Research

Search

Heuristic
Programming

Reasoning

Machine
Reasoning

Knowledge

Knowledge
Representation
Techniques

Directions

2 ARTIFICIAL INTELLIGENCE RESEARCH

Problem solving processes are a major research emphasis of AI. The approach of AI researchers is to study core concepts such as search, reasoning, and knowledge, and to design computer programs which are able to apply these concepts in problem solving processes. Studies of heuristic programming, machine reasoning, and knowledge representation techniques lead to a better understanding of human and machine problem solving processes. Since educators and trainers are constantly solving problems, studying problem solving methods, and teaching problem solving to others, AI research must be carefully examined by educators and trainers.

PROBLEM SOLVING IN THE FUTURE

The challenges of the information age and the changes predicted for the work force and schools of the 21st century require that educators and trainers become more proficient and efficient problem solvers and teachers of problem solving. According to AI researcher Roger Schank (1984):

> The theory-directed approach of Artificial Intelligence concerns the representation of knowledge, learning, and human thought processes. We are concerned with finding out what people know, how they know, and how they learn what they know. We are also interested in testing our theories of mind by constructing models of mental processes on a computer. (p. 32)

With easy access to information and its rapid creation, the need for knowledge representation techniques and an understanding of problem solving processes becomes increasingly critical. Will AI research, its results, and its knowledge representation techniques enable educators and trainers to be better problem solvers and teachers of problem solving processes in the 21st century?

AI research seeks solutions to difficult problems which cannot be achieved by existing processes and tools. Sokolowski (1988) describes the future impact of AI technology:

> In the case of any new technology, the new is first understood within the horizon set by the old. The earliest automobiles, for instance, looked very much like carriages. . . . Expert systems are the horseless carriages of artificial intelligence. They are analogous to the early writings that just recorded the content of the royal treasury or the distribution of the grain supply.
>
> This is not to belittle expert systems. The initial, small, obvious replacements for the old ways of doing things must settle in before the more distinctive accomplishments of a new intellectual form can take place—in this case, before the Dantes, Shakespeares, and Newtons, or the Jaguars, highways, and service stations of artificial intelligence can arise. (p. 50)

AI research seeks innovative processes and tools which will complement expert systems technology. Harmon, Maus, and Morrissey (1988) agree that:

> . . . several interesting AI techniques are still in the laboratories, not yet ready for commercial application. In some cases they await conceptual breakthroughs to become practical; in some cases they await the introduction of new hardware. What is certain is that AI labs will continue to provide innovations for the next decade or two. (p. 10)

If these judgments are correct, then educators and trainers who neglect this AI research will find themselves at an increasing disadvantage in understanding AI, cognitive science, computer science, and the knowledge advances that will accompany them. An understanding of the potential contribution of this infusion of AI technologies into education and training requires an exploration of AI problem solving research.

STUDIES OF PROBLEM SOLVING

AI concepts and techniques have emerged from research in human and machine intelligence and problem solving: areas where AI scientists continue to focus significant efforts. Examining the results of this AI research helps in understanding specific existing and proposed applications of AI technologies for education and training. AI and cognitive scientists use the term "problem solving" to describe almost all forms of cognition and intelligent behavior. AI research involves programming machines to solve many different problem types and to use different processes and strategies in those solutions. Intelligent machines must be able to use problem solving processes when presented with difficult and unique situations or else their usefulness will be limited.

Traditionally, AI research has studied complex tasks such as proving logical theorems, solving puzzles, and playing games such as chess to examine alternative approaches to problem solving. The study of these alternative approaches requires AI research in symbolic processing, heuristic programming, knowledge representation, and machine reasoning. Nearly all complex problems require these methods in their solutions whether the solver is human or machine (Hayes-Roth, 1985).

Problem solving in AI is by definition a set of purposeful and goal-directed behaviors. The solver of problems may be either a human or a computer. Problem solving involves analyzing a major goal into subgoals until a subgoal is defined which can be achieved through a direct action. The problem solving task involves finding a sequence of actions which transform the initial situation into successful attainment of the major goal. According to Newell and Simon (1972),

> To have a problem implies that certain information is given to the problem solver: information about what is desired, under what conditions, by means of what tools and operations, starting with what initial information, and with access to what resources.

The required content and sequence of actions needed to reach a solution (attain a major goal) are by definition unknown. The existence of a problem requires that:

1. An undesirable situation exists in the problem domain,
2. An initial situation is described,
3. A group of actions are possible
   (strategies, steps, procedures, moves), and
4. A goal situation is defined as the resolution of the problem
   (elimination of the unknown or dysfunctional situation).

Since more than one action is possible in a given situation, search is required to identify alternative actions before selecting one or more for application. The range of search strategies extends from the brute-force strategy of searching each alternative to heuristic strategies of searching by selective rule-of-thumb procedures.

SEARCH

Search is an area of research in both AI and computer science. Both humans and machines must seek and find information to effectively solve their problems. Research in AI involves studying approaches to searching for and retrieving knowledge and information. AI problem solving requires a search of alternative actions, choices, or solutions. In complex problem solving, the number of possible actions or solutions may be innumerable. *Search* is a major technique of AI which focuses on exploring possible situations and actions in the solution to a problem. Search is the process of starting at an initial situation and trying to reach a goal situation by evaluating possible alternative solutions. Search strategies comprise the control procedures which reduce time and decrease the memory capacity needed to solve specific problems. Search procedures require the efficient analysis and evaluation of the set of possible actions and solutions to find one or more acceptable solutions.

When individuals have a problem, they want to attain something and do not know what actions will be effective. In this problem solving situation, information is identified to clarify the goal and to establish a direction of search. Search then involves sorting through alternative courses of action to identify those which seem likely to lead to the goal. Search is determined by the task environment, the alternative actions available, and the internal representations of the problem. Every time a choice is made in a problem solving sequence, other possibilities are opened for new choices.

A *problem space* is the set of all possible choices or situations that can be generated from a given situation by each possible action. In a chess game, the problem space is the set of all possible moves and countermoves that can be generated in a given board situation. The vastness of this problem space limits the feasible use of brute-force search. Brute force search requires the program or individual to generate all possible moves from the beginning board position, explore all possible countermoves, and so on until a projected end of the game or goal situation was achieved. The major resource limits of time required to search this problem space and computer memory necessary for this large solution space makes this approach prohibitive given the current computer capabilities. Furthermore, human problem solvers who can work effectively in this problem space have demonstrated that brute force search is neither a necessary nor efficient strategy.

In a complex problem solving situation such as training an environmental technician, the trainer faces a similar challenge in the alternative actions possible in the design of instruction. For example, determining how to train the technician in the proper treatment of highly active, moving, and chemically unstable effluent before it enters a standard sewage treatment facility involves many possible choices and actions. As with the chess example, the possible situations defining the problem and solutions may or may not be known to the trainer. Even if known, the possibilities of training all possible actions leading to all possible situations required in a brute-force search would be impossible or inefficient.

Heuristic Search

Heuristics are techniques for solving AI problems through successive approximation. A heuristic is a rule of thumb which often, but not always, leads to a correct solution of a problem or type of problem (Anderson, 1985). *Heuristic search* allows the human or machine to use rules of thumb derived from experts to locate and retrieve knowledge, to simplify the problem, and to apply the most attractive subgoals or actions. Both humans and machines require heuristics to reduce the search space when problem space becomes increasingly complex. Since AI focuses on problems for which step-by-step procedures are unknown, heuristic search using approximation techniques provides a preferred solution strategy. Most real-world problems and decision making require heuristics for their simplification and solutions. AI scientists focus on heuristic search strategies to complement traditional computer systems and programs. Complex problems and real life situations demand solutions to "fuzzy and ill-structured" problems which may have infinitely large solution spaces (Simon, 1973). Problem solving to obtain the essentials of daily survival requires search strategies which allow for incorrect solutions and have a tolerance for error. Research in AI has made only minimal progress in producing effective problem solving strategies like those needed to successfully teach the computer to use the heuristic search strategies required to obtain the essentials for daily life.

HEURISTIC PROGRAMMING

Computer programs attempt to limit the search space by using heuristics to guide the search. *Heuristic programming* allows the computer to search for the most attractive solution, subgoal, or action. Heuristic programming encodes knowledge and search strategies which enable the computer to solve problems through successive approximation. AI researchers create and study the properties of heuristic programming to better understand both human and machine search behaviors. According to Clancey (1987):

> AI programming methods allow uncertain, heuristic knowledge to be efficiently represented so it can be easily modified and used for multiple purposes.

Heuristic programming is an exploratory computer-based approach to problem solving in which solutions are discovered by evaluating progressive actions toward the final solution (Rosenberg, 1986). For example, an AI program may be developed to enable the computer to search through a set of stored plausible solutions and select the best solutions by using heuristic rules from experts to test each hypothesized solution. Heuristic programming through hypothesis and testing does not always lead to a correct solution, but as in human decision making, incorrect answers are tolerated and partial solutions with projected confidence levels are deemed acceptable under the current practices of AI applications.

Heuristic programming is one AI method which clearly distinguishes AI from conventional computer programming. Conventional programming approaches require the use of algorithms which always seek the correct solution or only correct solutions. An algorithm is a set of processes for solving a problem in a finite number of steps in a fixed sequence (Gevarter, 1985). Algorithms are procedures, which when correctly carried out, result in solutions to the problem. For example, the procedure for adding numbers is an algorithm which will lead to correct summation. Computer science may be described as the study of the design, analysis, and application of algorithms (Arden, 1980). Some computer scientists have suggested that "heuristic programming" should be the term which replaces "artificial intelligence," since it better describes the approach of AI programming without the perceived connotations and misconceptions said to be associated with the AI label (Arden, 1980).

In addition to distinguishing AI from computer science approaches, the strategies of heuristic search and heuristic programming also highlight the cognitive relationships between problem solving processes, reasoning, and knowledge. The reasoning and knowledge of experts may be used to limit search. Heuristics of these experts may be programmed into the computer as rules which limit the possible actions or situations in the problem solving process. For example, AI scientists who attempt to develop computer chess programs study the heuristics of grand masters or expert chess players to reduce the problem space and improve the performance of these programs. Box 2.1 discusses the relationship between instructional design and problem solving.

Box 2.1

Instructional Design as Problem Solving

Design is a major category of problem solving which AI and cognitive scientists seek to improve in the future. All design sciences have three components: alternative goals, possibilities for action, and fixed constraints (Simon, 1983). For example, instructional design requires specification of outcomes, methods, and conditions of learning.

Instructional design is a discipline concerned with understanding how to teach. Systematic approaches to instructional design have only become a commonly understood and utilized practice in education and training during the past few years. A generally accepted gap between what is known from research and what is most frequently used in practice in education and training is thirty years. Nelson, Magliaro, and Sherman (1988) indicate that:

> Over the past three decades, instructional design has been characterized in a myriad of models which range from very specific, step-by-step algorithms to general frameworks or heuristics.
> (p. 29)

Educators and trainers need these general frameworks, heuristics, and algorithms to guide their decisions during the instructional design process.

By comparing instructional design to other problem solving processes, the research of AI and cognitive science can be used to generate implications for solving instructional problems encountered in education and training settings. Problems encountered in instructional design may be viewed as occurring along a continuum with "well-defined" problems on one end and "ill-defined" problems on the other (Greeno, 1976). Although the problems encountered during the process of instructional design may fall anywhere along this continuum, most problems have characteristics which assign them to the "ill-defined" end.

Some instructional designers advocate a structured, algorithmic approach to the development of instructional products. For example, a psychomotor training sequence may be designed through the step-by-step approach that outlines each incremental design activity (Annarino, 1983). Unfortunately, few problem areas are likely to be effectively analyzed and designed by algorithmic approaches.

Many designers indicate that most problems encountered by the instructional designer require heuristics for their solution. According to Nelson, Magliaro, and Sherman (1988):

> Because designers rarely have clear goals or structured behaviors to solve problems, they typically employ heuristics to guide, organize, or pattern problem solutions. (p. 30)

For example, instructional designers might use the following general heuristics to guide their decision-making: You should make decisions regarding the choice of media based upon consideration of the knowledge that comes from direct research results. This general heuristic would be effective in situations where the instructional designer could match the instructional problem with similar problems from research where a specific media demonstrated superiority. However, since most problems have unique characteristics, this general heuristic requires additional specific heuristics for the effective selection of media.

By studying general and specific heuristics of competent instructional designers, a better understanding of the design process will emerge. If general and specific heuristics used in solving instructional design problems could be captured in a machine, then specialized problem solving approaches would be available as a resource to instructional designers. In the meantime, the research from AI, cognitive science, and computer science with implications for instructional design should be carefully monitored and evaluated.

REASONING
Machine reasoning is a core area of AI study. Reasoning was initially the most intense area of AI exploration as researchers believed general reasoning strategies existed which would solve wide ranges of problems. Such quests in search of the Holy Grail are not unusual in emergent fields. That kind of single-mindedness by AI researchers likely resulted from their recognition of reasoning as a critical component in the ability to solve a diversity of problems. When a human or a machine reasons, it is able to deduce or verify knowledge and information beyond that which it has acquired or retrieved from memory (Barr & Feigenbaum, 1981). *Reasoning* is the process of drawing inferences, conclusions, and seeking analogies from an existing situation and from memory. Reasoning is the basis of all human mental activity and denotes several different kinds of activities. For example, individuals reason by drawing conclusions from a set of facts, making assumptions, organizing information, diagnosing possible causes, using analogies, and solving problems. Frequently, reasoning is used interchangeably as an identity for each and all of these processes.

Types of Reasoning
Problems may be solved by the following systems of reasoning:
1. Deductive,
2. Inductive, and
3. Analogical.

A major goal of AI research is to design computer programs that solve a broad range of problems by inductive, deductive, and analogical systems of reasoning.

Deductive Reasoning. Deduction is the attempt to find valid assertions which lead to valid conclusions. Deduction is a formal system in which symbols may be systematically combined in small steps under an established set of rules. The essence of deductive reasoning is the derivation of results or conclusions from valid statements. Deductive reasoning cannot use quantitative information or probability in reaching a conclusion.

Most expert systems presently use a deductive reasoning process. Although the deductive reasoning processes of educators and trainers do not rival those of the fictional detective, Sherlock Holmes, in their roles as diagnosticians, they are called upon to draw valid conclusions about their students and trainees from "reliable" and "valid" test results.

Inductive Reasoning. Induction is the attempt to find generalizations that describe or categorize a set of facts or body of information. Induction involves having a set of constraints to satisfy. The rules of inductive inference do not lead to necessarily valid conclusions. Inductive systems work at a big step or global level in problem solving. For example, educators and trainers must make the "big step" of deciding upon an instructional strategy based upon numerous observations of the student or trainee performing a large number of instructional tasks. This use of inductive reasoning seeks to achieve effective instruction within the constraints of the teaching situation.

Analogical Reasoning. The analogical approach to reasoning is qualitatively different from deductive and inductive approaches. Expert problem solvers commonly look for analogies and metaphors. Reasoning by analogy establishes a correspondence between elements of two systems, one known and one unknown. The known system is understood and the unknown system houses the problem or question of concern. Solutions to the concerns may be found by posing them in the known system. The major difficulty in analogical reasoning involves finding or defining correspondence between known and unknown systems that are valid and useful in terms of analogical reasoning. For example, an analogy has been made between coaching and teaching both in human and computer-based instruction. This analogy leads to possible changes in teaching based upon observations of effective coaches. However, if important differences exist (such as the different goals of teaching and coaching), then some changes resulting from analogical reasoning might be invalid or ineffective.

MACHINE REASONING

Machine reasoning requires the conversion of a given problem into an appropriate knowledge representation and reasoning formalism. Machines cannot be taught intuitive reasoning at present. Logical deduction is a reasoning formalism from which conclusions result when rules of reasoning are applied to true statements. Given appropriate programming, machines can emulate and perform logical deduction. The problems encountered in the implementation of logical deduction by a machine require that researchers clarify and codify reasoning procedures. This clarification process leads to improved understanding of human reasoning and logical deduction. Most current uses of machine reasoning in the workings of expert systems involve a simplified process of inference.

Inference Procedures

Inference is a subactivity of reasoning. Although the term "reasoning" and inference are sometimes used interchangeably in AI, most usage considers reasoning to involve rather lengthy sequences of inferences which focus on a main goal or problem. Inference is the process by which conclusions are drawn from facts and rules. During the inference process new facts may be derived from rules and known facts. The most frequently used inference method in AI is logical inference. Inductive, probabilistic, and statistical inferences are other kinds of machine reasoning which are used less frequently in AI research.

Inference Engines. Computer programs that perform inference are called inference engines. The inference engine uses the knowledge presented and information provided to draw conclusions and make recommendations about a problem presented to the computer system. According to Allen and Carter (1988):

> The hallmark of expert systems technology is the inference engine—a separate subsystem that contains strategies for making decisions and solving problems . . . the inference engine contains routines for deciding

which rules are relevant to the problem, how to apply the rules, and the order in which rules are executed. In short, the inference engine engages in a reasoning process by operating on propositions stored in the knowledge base. (p. 125)

A production system example shows how inference engines work and how inference is used in problem solving.

Production Systems. Rule-based systems which contain IF-THEN rule statements relating conditions and actions are called production systems. A production system consists of three components:
  1. Production rules,
  2. Working memory, and
  3. Rule interpreter.
Production rules are a technique for representing the knowledge required for problem solving. The production rules represent the knowledge base in a modular series of if-then statements.

Working memory consists of the data representing the current "state of the world" or collected information about the case. The working memory or short-term memory buffer of a production system stores the context of the situation (i.e. initial situation description). The *condition,* or left-hand side of the production rule, must be present in the working memory if the *action* (i.e. strategy, step, procedure, move) or right-hand side of the production rule is to "fire."

The rule interpreter is the controlling module that matches the information to the rules to determine the next rule to apply, or whether a rule is active. The rule interpreter is designed to decide action sequences. Most production systems use a phase and cycle approach to operation. The three phases are: matching, conflict resolution, and action. Matching involves comparing working memory to the condition portion of the rule (left-hand side). Conflict resolution is a sequence of decisions that determine which rule has priority if more than one rule is matched in working memory. Action may result in a change in working memory or a recommended action to the user of the production system. Cycles are repeated until appropriate actions are taken. In a production system with a large set of production rules, many cycles may be required prior to action recommendations.

KNOWLEDGE

Knowledge is a scarce resource whose refinement and representation results in successful problem solving. Knowledge enables individuals to behave intelligently and experts to solve difficult problems which cannot be solved by reasoning alone. Expert problem solvers achieve outstanding performance because of the knowledge they possess. Expert levels of problem solving depend on knowledge possessed and the ability to apply it. Recent AI research and development efforts have emphasized specific knowledge of the domain as the most important factor in successful problem solving. Although knowledge is of obvious importance, AI scientists' definition of knowledge is greatly limited in comparison to general dictionary definitions of knowledge which encompass "the body of truth, information, and principles acquired by mankind."

AI researchers define knowledge as stored symbols and information used by a person or machine to interpret, predict, and respond to a problem. *Knowledge* is the information, descriptions, relationships, and procedures a computer or person needs to solve problems and demonstrate intelligent behavior (Waterman, 1986). Knowledge is much more than information; it also implies organized information which is useable for solving problems (Harmon, Maus, & Morrissey, 1987). Knowledge may be defined as information that is "pared, shaped, interpreted, selected, and transformed" into a domain of expertise (Feigenbaum & McCorduck, 1983).

When AI researchers attempt to develop computer programs that solve difficult problems, knowledge is required for the program to emulate intelligent and expert performance. According to Barr and Feigenbaum (1981):

> We ascribe knowledge to programs in the same manner that we ascribe it to each other—based on observing certain behavior; we say that a program knows about objects in its domain, about events that have taken place, or about how to perform a specific task. (p. 143)

The pragmatic approach to knowledge used by the AI researcher is to improve the problem-solving behavior of the computer program through the addition of more usable knowledge.

Knowledge acquisition and retrieval are important study areas for understanding and improving human and machine intelligence. Effective problem solving results from the critical processes of knowledge acquisition and knowledge retrieval. Acquiring additional knowledge is required if one's problem solving strategies are to be improved. *Knowledge acquisition* is an integrative process relating new and old knowledge for efficient storage of information. *Knowledge retrieval* is a search process which determines what knowledge or information is relevant to a defined problem from a potentially huge knowledge base. Retrieval involves processes of establishing explicit links or connections between related representations of knowledge and grouping related representations of knowledge into larger structures. If several segments of knowledge are frequently used together, then they are combined for more effective retrieval, potential use in reasoning, and applications to similarly structured classes of problems. An understanding of knowledge acquisition and retrieval requires various classification systems for describing knowledge. Of the many and varied classifications of knowledge and their representations used by AI researchers in their work, some general types of knowledge may be considered for their usefulness in expert systems development and their application in education and training.

Types of Knowledge

AI researchers are centrally concerned with different types of knowledge which they identify as being required for effective problem solving to be accomplished by a computer-based intelligence. Barr and Feigenbaum (1982) classify the types of knowledge needed for intelligence under the terms: objects, events, performance, and meta-knowledge. Knowledge about objects includes representing classes, categories, and descriptions of objects. Event knowledge includes the representation of specific events, time sequences, and cause-effect relations. Performance knowledge consists of how to perform skills and do things. Knowledge representation consists of a language for describing things and a formalism for physically encoding the description (Fischler & Firschein, 1987). The following general types of knowledge must be represented if a machine is to behave knowledgeably and intelligently: domain knowledge, meta-knowledge, declarative knowledge, and procedural knowledge.

Domain Knowledge. The knowledge about a specified problem domain is obviously called domain knowledge. Existing AI programs are only able to provide consultation and teaching in narrowly defined problem domains. Domain knowledge is task-specific knowledge which is extracted from a human problem solver who knows how to solve specific problems in that domain. As indicated by Hayes-Roth (1983):

> Most of the world's challenging mental problems do not yield to general problem-solving strategies even when augmented with general efficiency heuristics. To solve problems in areas of human expertise such as engineering, medicine, or programming, machine problem solvers need to know what human problem solvers know about that subject. (p. 288)

Meta-knowledge. Knowledge about the use and control of domain knowledge involves meta or higher-order decision making; it is knowledge about knowledge. This knowledge in an AI program is not about the domain task itself, but knowledge about the structure of domain knowledge. Meta-knowledge is knowledge about the relationships of specific segments of knowledge to other segments of knowledge within the domain. Barr and Feigenbaum (1982) describe research in meta-knowledge:

> It is clear that researchers in AI and computer science will have to develop new techniques for handling the truly large-scale knowledge bases of the future. A step in this direction has been taken with the development of techniques for representing knowledge about knowledge, or meta-knowledge. (p. 85)

Current research in meta-knowledge is examining ways to determine how to organize large amounts of knowledge in a manner which is accessible and clear to the user. In addition, AI research is exploring ways in which meta-knowledge can evaluate the appropriateness and consistency of knowledge sources.

Declarative Knowledge. The facts, rules, and assertions represent or declare the knowledge that is known about the domain. Declarative knowledge is the "know-that" for a given domain. This declarative knowledge incorporates the concepts and relationships in the domain required for the solving of problems. Declarative knowledge is frequently more understandable and modular than the procedural knowledge of the domain. Both declarative and procedural uses of knowledge may achieve the same results, but one type of knowledge is often more efficient to utilize for a specific problem.

Procedural Knowledge. As indicated by its label, procedural knowledge is the type of knowledge which contains the step-by-step and heuristic procedures of the specific problem domain. Procedural knowledge is primarily a matter of "know-how" which refers to actions or what to do. Know-how and skills are almost synonymous. Know-how is so pervasive that it is frequently taken for granted. Know-how is learned through practice and experience. Application is required for maintaining know-how. Beginners or novices characteristically use know-that when they engage in problem solving. Experts use both know-how and know-that in problem solving.

KNOWLEDGE REPRESENTATION

Intelligence and problem solving depend upon the use of stored knowledge and information about objects, processes, goals, causality, time, and action. The study of knowledge, memory, symbols, and mental representations are areas of high interest for cognitive scientists and psychologists as well as AI researchers (Anderson, 1985). Cognitive science researchers have studied the representations used by people in the process of solving different types of problems.

Individuals report remembering knowledge as either hierarchical linear orderings of lists or visual-spatial structures that encode information and items. For example, studies demonstrate that individuals are able to access first and last items of a linear ordering more rapidly and easily any other ordered element. Meaning-based representations, according to research, show that individuals remember meaningful verbal and spatial information longer than exact wording or specific images (Anderson, 1985).

A remarkable attribute of human intelligence is the ability to convert a problem into a representation that allows for problem solving through a known process. This creative representation influences each individual's personal view of the world. Humans consciously and unconsciously use both formal and informal representation systems in their problem solving. Individuals are frequently unaware of their use of representations in problem solving or how that use affects their view of the world (Fischler & Firschein, 1987). Competent problem solvers are able to convert problems to representations which allow them to use familiar problem solving approaches. For example, a competent problem solver might draw a map from verbal directions to guide the search process in finding a specific location. Varied representations are used to facilitate problem solving processes.

Purposes of Knowledge Representation. A problem in AI is translated into a system for representing the types of knowledge and reasoning. Knowledge representation may consist of hierarchical, sequential, and spatial relationships with names, facts, procedures, and constraints. Models and languages are representations for describing the world. Logic and mathematical systems are also representations or formal languages for representing the world. For example, a natural language is a representational system which obviously has a language and a structure or syntax for both verbal descriptions and written communication.

One purpose of representations is to simplify a problem so that a goal may be accomplished or specific questions about a problem may be raised and answered. The careful selection of a representation is goal-directed (Fischler & Firschein, 1987). A person or machine must use a variety of knowledge representations to capture all aspects of the world. An effective representation allows a given problem to be translated into another representation or problem type that has a known solution. Other roles for representation are to improve interpretation, prediction, deduction, and organization. Problem solvers interpret, organize, predict, deduce, and question based upon their representation of knowledge.

One important aspect of intelligence is the ability to create and manipulate representations effectively. According to Fischler and Firschein (1987),

> The concept of representation as a way of selectively, and even creatively modeling the world, has proven to be one of the key ideas underlying our understanding of both human and machine intelligence. (p. 67)

Current AI research includes significant efforts which seek to discover, explicate, and apply knowledge representation techniques to enhance problem solving processes. Success in these endeavors would be important for educators and trainers who have long recognized the ability of an individual to a convert novel problem situation into a representation that allows its solution. Attempts to represent knowledge in the computer have led to a better understanding of human representation. Knowledge representation involves the design of knowledge structures for storing information in computer programs as well as development of procedures for manipulating these knowledge structures (Barr & Feigenbaum, 1981).

Types of Knowledge Representation Techniques

Computers require that knowledge be represented in a structured and explicit system before ordered storage, retrieval, and inference making can occur (Fischler & Firschein, 1987). Knowledge must be represented in a formal notation or data structure that the machine can manipulate during retrieval, inference making, or storage in memory.

This may be accomplished through varied knowledge representation techniques. Each type of representation technique is useful or efficient for specific purposes. Choosing one type of representation technique facilitates some operations and makes others inefficient. Evaluation of representation techniques might involve an examination of modularity, primitive elements, and ease of encoding (Barr & Feigenbaum, 1981).

The type of knowledge representation technique used must be selected prior to encoding because the structure of knowledge will greatly influence problem solving. Knowledge representation techniques focus on the form or structure of the knowledge, yet no single representation technique is likely to capture all aspects of a real object, event, or problem and no technique is necessarily better for all situations, objects, or problems. The selected knowledge representation techniques should be stable and require little change even though the represented situation changes slightly. Compact size of representations should be promoted to limit redundant information and to bring parsimony in search strategies (Fischler & Firschein, 1987). While various formalisms or knowledge representation techniques have been used in AI research and expert systems development, only a limited number of representational techniques or schemes are described in AI literature (Fischler & Firschein, 1987; Barr & Feigenbaum, 1981). Each knowledge representation technique may serve different functions in AI research. Rules, frames, decision trees, semantic nets, and direct representation are knowledge representation techniques commonly used in expert systems and ICAI research.

Rules. The most common knowledge representation technique presently used in expert systems development is the rule, sometimes called the production rule. The most important aspect of representation in a production system, as previously described, is the production rule. Rules are used to model a wide range of problem solving behaviors in rule-based programs called production systems. Rules are a knowledge representation technique for specifying recommendations, directives, and strategies. The usage of the term "rule" in knowledge representation is more specific than its lay usage or specialized usage in education and training. In knowledge representation, rules are conditional statements with two parts. The form of the production rule is *condition-action* pairs in the form "IF this *condition* or premise holds, THEN this *action* or conclusion is appropriate" (Barr & Feigenbaum, 1981). The IF clauses establish conditions which must apply if the THEN clauses are to be acted upon. The clauses of rules are usually made up of objects, attributes, and values.

Rules may be very simple or extremely complex. A simple rule might be "If the light is red, then stop." The terms "and" and "or" add complexity to rules. For example "If the light is red or yellow and your car is approaching the intersection, then stop or take your chances." Rules may have uncertainty attached to either a clause or the rule itself. Uncertainty is a value less than definite that the clause or rule is true. For example, a person might be unsure that a coin will become heads (.5) or confident about a choice (.9).

Rules are important AI concepts which are used in expert system development and modeling human problem solving (Fischler & Firschein, 1987). Rules are most often used in expert systems development because they can be easily used to represent a large body of specific and real world knowledge (Barr & Feigenbaum, 1981). Rules are also used in the development of models of cognition because of the similarity between stimulus-response relationships and production rules (Anderson, 1985). One obvious advantage of rules as a knowledge representation technique is the modularity of production rules as "pieces of knowledge" (Barr & Feigenbaum, 1981). This modularity of rules allows for developing large knowledge bases necessary to capture expertise. This rule-based approach to problem solving complements the specific approaches of educators and trainers. For example, Gagne (1985) emphasizes the use of rules in the problem solving process:

> Problem solving may be viewed as a process by which the learner discovers a combination of previously learned rules which can be applied to achieve a solution for a novel situation. (p. 155)

Rules as an important AI knowledge representation technique are compatible with rule analysis approaches of instructional design which are so useful in education and training. Rules or production rules are considered in this section of the chapter and inference and control in a production system will be considered later in the chapter. Chapter 4 will discuss the use of uncertain rules and rule-based systems in the development of expert systems.

Frames. One important way of representing knowledge about objects and events is through the use of frames. A frame is a data structure which contains knowledge hooks or slots for all information associated with the object or event. Slots store elements or values for a given situation. Slots may include default values, pointers to other frames, sets of rules, or sets of procedures for attaining values. Slots are similar to fields in a data base with the extended power of also containing rules, graphic information, explanatory information, questions to ask, or the capability of inferring new information. Frames are a unique representation technique which allow for the inclusion of both declarative knowledge about objects or events, and procedural attachments which specify how values are to be obtained (Harmon & King, 1985). For example, a generic frame for a student might have slots for name, sex, IQ score, and an attached procedure for determining the student's interest in the content of instruction for an ICAI system. When a specific student interacts with the ICAI system, knowledge is stored in the frame until retrieved or needed for reasoning about the student.

One way to improve on a rule-based system is to include frames which more easily model causal knowledge. Frames are a template or generic pattern for representing related knowledge about a narrow subject. Related knowledge is grouped into frames and frames can be connected to other frames or rules. Frames are related hierarchically—that is frames may contain subframes which may contain other subframes. According to Rauch-Hindin (1988):

> . . . the frame-based organization comes closer to modeling real-world systems and mimicking the way human beings reason about the world. (p. 73)

Frames are particularly useful in knowledge domains which cluster around objects, concepts, or events. For example, training in medicine tends to cluster around diseases or education in history tends to cluster around world events. Figure 2.1 shows a frame adapted from the machine learning program called AM.

NAME: Prime Number
DEFINITION:
    ORIGIN: Number-of-divisors-of (x) = 2
    ITERATIVE: (for x > 1) : For i from 2 to sqrt (x), -(i / x)
EXAMPLES: 2, 3, 5, 7, 11, 13, 17
    BOUNDARY: 2, 3
    BOUNDARY FAILURES: 0, 1
    FAILURES: 12
SPECIALIZATIONS: Odd Primes, Prime Pairs, Prime Uniquely-addables
ANALOGIES:
    Maximally divisible numbers are converse extremes of
    Number-of-divisors-of,
    Factor a nonsimple group into simple group

FIGURE 2.1 Frame Representation of Prime Concept
(Adapted from AM machine learning program
shown in Cohen and Feigenbaum, 1982)

Decision Trees. Graphic representations are used to show all possible consequences which can result from an initial situation through a series of branching lines. These graphic representations are called decision or search trees. One approach to representing a complex problem and alternative choices in AI is a decision tree. To search the tree, the computer starts with an initial condition and branches with each decision. "Blind" methods for searching require an orderly sequence of trying each solution branch of the tree. Alternative search approaches are needed for the solution to difficult problems because the number of branches becomes computationally impossible or far too time consuming to search. Decision trees are a useful representation for exploring alternatives in a decision support system when decisions are quite simple. However, most real-world situations require that decisions involve multiple factors. Most present uses of decision trees focus on game situations such as chess moves or AND/ OR graphing situations such as those used in finite mathematics. A game tree for tic-tac-toe would represent all possible alternatives. A thorough discussion of search and decision trees is provided by Barr and Feigenbaum (1981). A decision tree may be considered as a type of hierarchical semantic network.

Semantic Net.   A semantic or relational net (network) is used to describe relationships between "things" for the purpose of general question answering (Fischler & Firschein, 1987). A net consists of nodes and links between nodes which represent interrelationships (Barr & Feigenbaum, 1981). Nodes represent the important objects, concepts, or events usually by a box or circle. Links are lines with explicit labels such as "is a," "is one of," or "belongs to." The major advantage of semantic nets is their simplicity and flexibility.

The purpose of semantic nets is to show relationships between "things" and to clearly represent relationships. For example, a simple fact or association between Brazil and its classification is the statement BRAZIL IS A COUNTRY in a semantic net.   Semantic nets were first used as a model of human associate memory. Semantic nets were used in the first ICAI program, SCHOLAR, to represent geographic knowledge about South American countries and cities.

Although few formal procedures are specified for semantic nets, some structure is required to improve communictation. Without some hierarchical structure, complex semantic nets may become tangles or meshes which are difficult to understand or use. Organizing a semantic net into a hierarchy allows for better communication and validation (Carrico, Girard, & Jones, 1989). For example, COUN-TRY may become the highest node with BRAZIL and CHILE as lower nodes on the organizational chart. Semantic nets may be converted into decision trees in which the nodes represent goals and the links represent explicit decisions when appropriate (Carrico, Girard, & Jones, 1989).

Direct (Analogical) Representation. Direct representation can be defined as a representation technique in which the properties of parts and the relations between parts correspond to the object and parts represented (Barr & Feigenbaum, 1981). Direct or analogical representations are diagrams, maps, or models which denote the structural and metric relation to some of the properties of the situation or object being represented in a natural way. The terms "iconic" and "isomorphic" representations are frequently used as synonyms for direct and analogical representations (Fischler & Firschein, 1987). For example, a city map directly represents the streets in the relational distances between points on the map and corresponding distances between places in the city.

In direct or analogical representations, problems are solved by completing a set of experimental procedures on the representation similar to the step by step procedures of a physical experiment. The problem constraints need not be explicitly represented in direct representations. Direct representation is used as a representation technique in computational vision research. With the increasing use of graphics and iconic representation on microcomputers, direct representation will be a useful technique in education and training. For example, in the program called "The Electric Cadaver," a medical student accesses information on diagrams of the human anatomy by pointing and clicking with a mouse device on the point of interest (Coale, 1989). Hypermedia environments and multimedia programs, as discussed in Chapter Five, use direct representations for providing access to specific information.

CHAPTER SUMMARY

• Artificial Intelligence (AI) involves the study of problem solving, search, reasoning, and knowledge representation. Intelligence is defined for purposes of AI research as the ability to solve novel and difficult problems. AI researchers seek the solution to problems through the processes of systematic analysis and the use of computers as tools.

• Problem solving in AI is defined as purposeful and goal-directed behaviors. Major goals are analyzed to determine subgoals and actions which lead to goal attainment and the problem's resolution.

• Search is an area of AI and computer science research which explores efficient approaches for finding and retrieving knowledge and information. Heuristic search is a successive approximation technique which uses knowledge and rules of thumb derived from experts to simplify problems.

• Heuristic programming is an exploratory computer-based approach in which solutions are discovered by evaluating actions toward the final solution. In heuristic programming, the computer efficiently searches for the best or most attractive solutions, subgoals, or actions. Heuristic programming distinguishes AI from computer science by using encoded knowledge in problem solving. Heuristic programming may be contrasted with algorithmic approaches of conventional computer programming.

• Reasoning is the basis for all human mental activities. Reasoning is the process of drawing inferences, conclusions, and seeking analogies. Inductive, deductive, and analogical reasoning are types of reasoning studied by AI researchers. Research on human and machine reasoning has led to a better understanding of problem solving and inference procedures.

• Machine reasoning is a core area of AI research. Inference procedures are frequently used in machine reasoning. Production systems are a type of inference system commonly used to control reasoning in an expert system.

• Knowledge is required for problem solving, expertise, decision making, consulting, and teaching. AI and cognitive scientists study knowledge to understand and reconstruct human and machine representations. The study of the relationships of knowledge to other constructs provides direction for clarifying, codifying, and communicating knowledge. Experts are able to convert problems to a knowledge representation which allows them to use a familiar problem solving approach. AI researchers are centrally concerned with domain knowledge, meta-knowledge, declarative knowledge, and procedural knowledge.

• Knowledge representation techniques are used to structure knowledge in AI research and development. The following knowledge representation techniques have been frequently used in AI research: production rules, frames, semantic nets, decision trees, and analogical representations.

• Rules are the most common type of knowledge representation techniques presently used in expert systems development. The form of the production rule is IF the condition or premise holds, THEN this action or conclusion is appropriate. Rules may have uncertainty or confidence values attached to them.

SCORECARD				
Will AI Research and Development Efforts Contribute to Education and Training?				
Topics	Question Dimensions			
	Feasibility	Improved Effectiveness	Capacity Enhancing	Future Utility
Problem Solving				
Search				
Heuristic Programming				
Reasoning				
Machine Reasoning				
Knowledge				
Knowledge Representation				

Comments:

DIRECTIONS

Research may be viewed as the ability to discern and resolve a problem using the information and knowledge presently available. Research is essentially a simple process, but the complexities of research become quickly apparent as we attempt to understand not only the research of our own disciplines, but especially the research of other disciplines. Understanding research in your own discipline can often be difficult. Few practitioners enjoy reading research studies in their professional journals. Determining how to apply these findings is an additional challenge. When you encounter research from another discipline the challenge is increased. New concepts and processes of the new discipline must be mastered if this research is to be understood and effectively applied.

AI is primarily an interdisciplinary area of research which requires an understanding of many new concepts and processes. In addition, many of the concepts such as knowledge, information, reasoning, and communication are defined differently in AI than in education. In the distant future, major areas of AI research are likely to contribute to training and education. However, understanding current AI research, findings, and directions is a major challenge to educators and trainers. Research and the findings from AI do not readily transfer. At the same time, major variables of interest such as knowledge and expertise have overlap with those central to education and training. Since knowledge and expertise are so critical to education and training, we predict that AI research will result in capacity enhancing developments for the near and distant futures.

Problem solving is a critical process of education and training. Studying human or artificial intelligence has apparent value to educators and trainers; we need to understand the problem solving processes of our students to instruct them effectively. In addition, we need to understand experts'

problem solving processes in order to design effective instruction which simultaneously enables our students to achieve
specific objectives and improves their capabilities to learn.
Problem solving is a major goal for education. Applying
problem solving skills in real-world settings is a goal of
training and education. Intelligence is required for solving the
novel problems encountered during the process of education.
Effective training will result from an improved understanding
of problem solving processes.

AI research efforts regarding problem solving can contribute to the expertise of professionals and enable that expertise to be captured and used through expert systems for the
improvement of education and training processes and outcomes. As the problem solving processes become better
understood through AI research and development, these findings can be applied to problems in education and training. Just
as research with naive and handicapped learners contributes to
a better understanding of all learners, research with naive
machines will contribute to our understanding of both naive
and sophisticated learners. To be successful, AI researchers
must program these naive machines carefully through each
step in the process of problem solving or decision making.
Both human and machine problem solvers require extensive
and high quality knowledge and precise use of that knowledge
for effective problem solving.

Search is an intriguing aspect of problem solving. As
educators and trainers, we frequently must search through
large amounts of information to find the specific information
that we need to teach or use. Heuristic search strategies are
employed both consciously and unconsciously in this process.
Heurisitic programming uses computers to seek alternative
solutions to difficult and novel problems through a process of
successive approximation. If heuristic programming is feasible, then computers will become even more valuable search
tools. At present, many educators and trainers use computers

and traditional database procedures in their search for information. If AI research is successful, "intelligent" computers using heuristic programming and search techniques will provide better information and knowledge in more time efficient fashion than is currently possible.

Whether applied in an education or training context, the design of instruction usually represents a heuristic activity. Formative evaluation is a technique used to assess the effects of progressive actions toward the final design and effective instruction. The heuristic search and programming activities of AI parallel those of instructional design. Interactions between AI researchers and instructional designers focused on the cross-field adaption of their respective heuristic searching and programming techniques would likely result in improvements for both sets of experts. The precision required in heuristic programming plus its domain knowledge dependency could be used to improve and complement instructional design techniques. Another perhaps less obvious, but equally fruitful application would be the preplanning of activities where socioeconomic, experiential, and cognitive style information about the learner could be subjected to heuristic programming techniques so educators and trainers would have a more precise understanding of those learners.

At the same time, the AI researcher's abilities to structure machine control heuristic programming strategies would be enhanced by capturing the heuristics revealed in interactions with educators and trainers and applying them in attempts to effectively represent problem and decision aspects, respectively, in AI research and development.

In surveying current AI literature, it appears that interaction between AI researchers and educational researchers would prove mutually beneficial. For example, educators and trainers could profit from the knowledge taxonomies and knowledge representation techniques of AI researchers. In instruction, domains of knowledge are most frequently differentiated by theoretical types of learning such as Gagne's domains of learning or the structures of academic disciplines.

Unfortunately, the term "knowledge" is not being used in a manner consistent with previous uses of the term by individuals unfamiliar with computer science or AI. Knowledge has unfortunately achieved an ill-defined, buzz word status in AI. The term "knowledge" has been used as a descriptor to form many other AI terms such as knowledge systems, knowledge representation, knowledge acquisition, knowledge networks, and knowledge-based expert systems. Knowledge has positive connotations that imply intelligence and understanding. Knowledge is frequently used to replace the terms "information" and "intelligent" in AI and computer science such as in knowledge processing and knowledge technology. This replacement is due to the commercial success of expert systems and the expanding capabilities of computers to represent symbolic relationships rather than just information and numerical data.

Knowledge representation is a potentially exciting concept for educators and trainers. Rarely, we suspect, do educators and trainers consider the question and its implications—"If I want someone to learn this, how can I most effectively represent it?" The representation of knowledge in a computer requires adequate answers to this question. Most educators and trainers fail to consciously examine the knowledge representation techniques used in textbooks and manuals or the accompanying limiting or enhancing effects they hold for learners. Can abstract concepts which are usually defined, identified, and exemplified in text form be more functionally represented for some learners in graphic from? Are the concepts of war, revolution, responsibility, additive property, and interdependence more effectively represented for instruction in graphic format? Can a result of learning, like "chunking" knowledge into meaning-associated networks, be used to predesign knowledge representation across disciplines, subject areas, or job function areas? Should educators and trainers consciously array knowledge prior to instruction? We think so. Rather than accepting knowledge for instruction in the passive formats represented by textbooks, workbooks, review exercises, and worksheets, educators and trainers can use knowledge engineering techniques to design knowledge representation formats which promote effectiveness in specific instructional contexts. Knowledge representation is an arena of fruitful interaction between those addressing the demands of effective education and training and those developing the techniques of knowledge engineering.

Rarely do educators and trainers consider knowledge in terms of cross-functions of different types of domains as in AI. AI researchers, on the other hand, could gain more functional growth in knowledge by applying their methodologies to the real-world problems of education and training. Through the interaction required for both fields to gain these ends, mutually satisfying results would be likely to enhance their respective capacities and add more effective techniques to their domains of practice.

Knowledge is a powerful concept in education and training. Knowledge is both an essential means to education and a necessary end. Competent educators and training specialists must have knowledge of content, of their students, and how to teach in order to enable them to productively use or overcome the characteristics and demands of educational and performance environments. A major purpose of education and training is to convey knowledge and to establish its utility.

TOPICAL REFERENCES

Problem Solving

Amarel, S. (1987). Problem solving. In S.C. Shapiro (Ed.) *Encyclopedia of artificial intelligence*. New York: John Wiley & Sons.

Pearl, J. (1984). *Heuristics: Intelligent strategies for computer problem solving*. Reading, MA: Addison-Wesley Publishing.

Rubinstein, M.F. (1975). *Patterns of problem solving*. Englewood Cliffs, NJ: Prentice- Hall.

Search

Barr, W., & Feigenbaum, E.A. (Eds.) (1981). *Handbook of artificial intelligence–Vol. I.* Los Altos, CA: William Kaufmann, Inc.

Reasoning

Anderson, J.R. (1985). *Cognitive psychology and its implications*. San Francisco: W.H. Freeman.

Henschen, L. (1987). Reasoning. In S.C. Shapiro (Ed.) *Encyclopedia of artificial intelligence*. New York: John Wiley & Sons.

Machine Reasoning

Cohen, P.R., & Feignenbaum (Eds.) (1982). *Handbook of Artificial Intelligence–Vol. III*. Los Altos, CA: William Kaufmann, Inc.

Fischler, M.A., & Firschein, O. (1987). *Intelligence: The eye, the brain, and the computer*. Reading, MA: Addison-Wesley Publishing.

Knowledge

Anderson, J. R. (1985). *Cognitive psychology and its implications.* San Francisco: W.H. Freeman.

Hayes-Roth, F., & Waterman, D.A. (1983). *Building expert systems.* Reading, MA: Addison-Wesley Publishing.

Fischler, M.A., & Firschein, O. (1987). *Intelligence: The eye, the brain, and the computer.* Reading, MA: Addison-Wesley Publishing.

Knowledge Representation Techniques

Barr, W., & Feigenbaum, E.A. (Eds.) (1981). *Handbook of artificial Intelligence–Vol. I.* Los Altos, CA: William Kaufmann, Inc.

Fischler, M.A., & Firschein, O. (1987). *Intelligence: The eye, the brain, and the computer.* Reading, MA: Addison-Wesley Publishing.

Harmon, P., & King, D. (1985). *Expert systems--Artificial intelligence in business.* New York: John Wiley & Sons.

Kramer, B.M., & Mylopoulos, J. (1987). Knowledge representation. In S.C. Shapiro (Ed.) *Encyclopedia of artificial intelligence.* New York: John Wiley & Sons.

Waterman, D.A. (1986). *A guide to expert systems.* Reading, MA: Addison-Wesley Publishing.

Knowledge Map of Chapter Three
Knowledge Engineering

Transfer of Expertise

Knowledge Engineering

Expert Systems Development
> **Plan**
> **Design**
> **Construct Prototype**
> **Evaluate**

AI Tools
> **Hardware**
> **AI Languages**
> **Expert Systems**
> > **Development Tools**

Directions

3 KNOWLEDGE ENGINEERING

Knowledge engineering is a field of AI research and development which explores knowledge acquisition and utilization. Knowledge engineers develop expert systems and intelligent computer-assisted instruction (ICAI) systems. Expert systems development processes and tools are useful for developing these computer-based systems through a systematic approach of planning, design, prototype construction, and evaluation. The role of the knowledge engineer is complementary to that of the instructional designer. A concurrent development process of knowledge engineering and instructional design can result in the clarification of knowledge and the transfer of expertise and can elicit more effective results than can either process functioning alone.

TRANSFER OF EXPERTISE IN THE FUTURE

In the future, knowledge will be clarified and expertise transferred through the use of AI processes and tools. Edward Feigenbaum and Pamela McCorduck (1983) in their controversial book, *The Fifth Generation,* have enthusiastically described the impact of knowledge engineering on information and knowledge:

> The computer is the main artifact of the age of information. Its purpose is certainly to process information—to transform, amplify, distribute, and otherwise modify it. But more important, the computer *produces* information. The essence of the computer revolution is that the burden of producing the future knowledge of the world will be transferred from human head to machine artifacts. (p. 40)

Fredrick Hayes-Roth, Donald Waterman, and Douglas Lenat (1983), pioneers in the development of expert systems, indicate that:

> Machines that lack knowledge seem doomed to perform intellectually trivial tasks. Those that embody knowledge and apply it skillfully seem capable of equaling or surpassing the best performance of human experts. Knowledge provides the power to do work; knowledge engineering is the technology that promises to make knowledge a valuable industrial commodity. (p. 3)

If the predictions of these knowledge engineers are correct, AI processes and tools will significantly impact the acquisition and utilization of knowledge. Donald Waterman (1986) in *A Guide to Expert Systems* indicates that:

> The accumulation and codification of knowledge is one of the most important aspects of an expert system. (p. 7)

The knowledge engineering process is a useful activity which makes heuristic knowledge explicit and accessible. In the future, knowledge and expertise will be explicit, accumulated, codified, and accessible.

Knowledge acquisition and utilization processes are described as useful processes by educators and trainers. For example, Alan Hofmeister and Margaret Lubke (1986), developers of expert systems in education, indicate that:

> The process of assembling and organizing knowledge bases for expert systems is a productive activity in its own right. The development of the "if-then" rules of a knowledge base clarifies existing knowledge and identifies areas where knowledge is needed.

However, knowledge engineering is a new area of AI research and development which still requires careful study. An important question for educators and trainers is: How can computers and humans work together to effectively transfer knowledge and expertise?

TRANSFER OF EXPERTISE

Expertise has a central role in the present technological society. *Expertise* is the body of knowledge which underlies the ability of experts to solve problems and make decisions. It consists of public and private knowledge. Public knowledge is the published theories, definitions, and information included in the books, journals, and references of the domain. Private knowledge allows human experts to identify "promising approaches" to problems, make "educated guesses," and to cope with "incomplete or errorful data" (Hayes-Roth, Waterman, & Lenat, 1983). Expertise requires a large amount of heuristic and procedural knowledge. This knowledge results in consistently high performance levels by domain experts which most others seem unable to achieve. Expertise must be transferred from these domain experts to other members of society.

A *domain expert* is an individual who is able to solve both common and novel problems in a specialized area or domain because of education, training, and experience (Waterman, 1986). The term "expert" connotes someone who can solve problems in his or her specialized sphere of knowledge and information. According to Hayes-Roth, Waterman, and Lenat (1983) in *Building Expert Systems:*

> One feature of expertness is that it usually comes in *narrow, specialized domains.* For example, it is easy to imagine an expert in almost any technical field (say, mass spectrometry or protein crystallography), but not in such everyday activities as understanding natural language or visual scenes. (p. 42)

It takes time for experts to gain experience and learn the specialized knowledge in a domain. Studies show that domain knowledge makes the difference between successful and unsuccessful problem solving, not native intelligence or general reasoning ability. Experts in a domain are not necessarily intelligent in other areas of problem solving. Expertise does not necessarily generalize from domain to domain (Anderson, 1985). Areas such as chess and mathematics require many years of practice to attain expert levels of performance.

Experts, regardless of specialized domain, have many common characteristics. They have competence which declines smoothly when given difficult problems departing from their domain of expertise. They demonstrate a knowledge of the limits of their expertise by indicating when and how to solve a problem and indicating when a problem is outside their expertise. Experts have the ability to explain "what" and "why" when solving problems. Experts have the ability to select appropriate models for problem solving and can use these models in effective decision making. They represent problems in terms of abstract features or models which are predictive of solutions. Experts use efficient search strategies. They have the ability to reorganize strategies and information when necessary. This allows them to analyze well-formulated problems in an efficient manner (Harmon and King, 1985).

Domain experts are individuals with a high degree of knowledge and skill in their area of specialization which allows them to make fine discriminations in applying what they know. These domain experts must study perceived patterns and associated solutions in the problems they encounter on a daily basis. They must remember a remarkable number of cases, situations, or examples. Domain experts possess uncanny conscious and subconscious abilities to make fine distinctions in problem solving situations and environments. They make effective distinctions regarding relevant and irrelevant information from their own knowledge base. They know important and rare facts as well as effective, generalizable strategies. Most importantly, experts are able to select knowledge from their expertise which matches the demands of an identified problem situation, and therefore are able to solve problems efficiently and effectively while novices are unable to make such connections.

Research in AI and cognitive science which compares expert and novice problem solving behaviors has shown significant and important differences. The expertise of computer programmers, physicists, and mathematicians has been studied to determine differences between experts' and novices' problem solving. Box 3.1 discusses chess expertise as an exemplary area of expertise research. Box 3.2 describes issues related to replicating this expertise research in the area of instructional design

Box 3.1
Chess Expertise

Computer chess playing programs with varying levels of expertise are commercially available for most microcomputers. These computerized chess programs frequently attract attention because most people perceive chess playing to require high levels of intelligence and expertise. Chess was one of the first games selected to challenge AI research because of its complexity. Chess research has generated many AI concepts and techniques.

Expertise research in chess playing often compares the playing of chess experts to that of novices. Some studies encourage novices and experts to describe their thought processes orally and then use protocol analysis to enable better understanding of decision making. Novices have common patterns and problems in trying to acquire chess expertise. Novices learn basic rules for playing such as "do not allow opponent to take your piece unless you can exchange for a piece of equal value." The novice does not know when these rules should be violated or in which situations they do not hold true. They lack a coherent understanding of the game and perform by following simple rules and avoiding mistakes. Novices must concentrate to avoid making mistakes. For example, they cannot carry on a conversation or attend to higher level advice and maintain effective performance. The computer can easily outperform the novice at chess because of its memory for rules and speed in simple decision making.

A chess grand master is a domain expert who has a record of solving chess problems and defeating opponents in tournaments involving other chess experts. Grand masters spend a minimum of ten years studying and playing games. Studies indicate that these grand masters have accurate memories of over 50 thousand patterns which relate groups of chess pieces. Although adequate memory ability is obviously of importance, native intelligence is not a substitute for study and experience in chess problem solving.

Grand masters significantly differ from novices in their approaches to problem solving in the domain of chess. Chess masters store the solutions to many problems that a novice would consider novel. Novices must analyze the different patterns, try to project the consequences, and then decide on a best move. By having the solutions in memory, the chess master can focus on strategies and not make errors. Some chess masters are able to simultaneously play two games while blindfolded because of the patterns and memories they are able to store.

One example of research on chess expertise involved comparisons between the visual memory of chess masters and novices. To study the differences in visual memory, both novices and chess masters were exposed to meaningful and random board positions. Chess masters reported remembering the positions of chunks of four or five pieces when given meaningful board positions. Chess masters were able to reconstruct the positions of 20 pieces after only 5 seconds of study. In contrast, novice chess players could remember only five pieces. Research with randomly placed individual pieces revealed that there was no difference between novice and grand master memories for position. This finding is consistent with research results on the efficiency of chunking information in memory (DeGroot, 1965).

One similarity between novice and expert chess players is that they both consider about the same number of alternatives before selecting a move. The differences between experts and novice players are not the number of branches explored, but the exploration of branches with the most potential. Chess masters have a repertoire of positions for which the move is immediately obvious so that they can play at a high rate of speed. Expert moves are triggered "automatically." Difficult strategies such as those required in fast moving or lightning chess show immediate differences between novice and advanced players.

Although computer chess playing programs can defeat most advanced chess playing opponents, they are unable to defeat grand masters because the expertise used by grand masters cannot be captured in a machine at the present time. Computers have not been effectively taught to reason with meaningful configurations or patterns which are within the expertise of grand masters. Although computers can efficiently search through thousands of moves in the amount of time a person searches less than a hundred moves, grand masters defeat computer programs because looking ahead and searching is only one part of chess playing. Exhaustive search of all possible moves is impossible. Recent studies have been focused on the heuristic search strategies of chess experts since alternative strategies and choices in most fields of endeavor are nearly infinite. Efficient chess-playing computer programs use heuristic search to narrow the number of alternatives explored, but as yet cannot match the performance of grand masters in selecting the move with the most potential.

Studies of transfer of chess expertise through computer consultation or teaching would be of great interest to educators and trainers. Chess expertise as captured on the computer has usefulness as a consulting and teaching system to novice and intermediate players. The commercial success of chess playing computer programs demonstrates that many individuals are purchasing and utilizing these programs as learning tools. Studies of the transfer of expertise should logically result from the continuing facination with chess as a subject of AI research. A major problem to be solved in transfer of expertise is the difference between human and machine strategies. For example, the computer's capabilities of looking ahead hundreds of moves does not transfer to an effective human strategy. Development of systems which can transfer expertise, therefore, must focus upon capabilities which humans consistently demonstrate.

Box 3. 2

Instructional Design Expertise

There is a great need for research on transferring expertise in education and training. Major challenges for education and training are to transfer expertise from expert to novice and from research into practice. Within education and training, an understanding of instructional design expertise will improve instruction. Instructional design is an important domain within education and training that can be improved by the comparative study of thought processes and decision making of novice and expert designers.

Interest in decision making in the classroom has increased as researchers attempt to understand the thought processes of educators and trainers. For example, Cauderhead (1981) compared beginning to experienced teachers in terms of their responses to descriptions of common critical incidents. He found a marked difference in the nature and sophistication of their interpretations and understanding of classroom events when he analyzed the responses of both groups of teachers. Beginning teachers did not seem to extract the same kind or level of meaning from the descriptions. Fogarty, Wang, and Creek (1982) have supported the findings that experienced and novice teachers differ considerably in their perceptions of classroom events. It is hypothesized that this difference in perception may lead to differences in decision making. Few studies have been conducted which attempted to train teachers in decision making skills. However, recent interest has resulted in several approaches to this complex process. Improvement has focused on developing knowledge about effective teaching and translating it into algorithms that teachers can learn and incorporate into their planning prior to teaching (Brody, 1979).

Novice teachers have difficulty effectively applying their knowledge of instructional design in complex, real-world settings of education and training. According to Nelson, Magliaro, and Sherman (1988):

> Novice designers are more likely to use design models at a surface level. (p. 33)

Novice designers miss subtleties and focus only on basic procedures required for effective design. They reveal slavish dependence upon the procedural rather than strategic aspects of various design models.

Educators and trainers who demonstrate the highest levels of expertise must be studied to determine their decision making and problem solving strategies during both planning and instruction. The effectiveness of teaching expertise might be demonstrated by student achievement, engaged time, and productivity. For example, *The Handbook of Research on Teaching* (Wittrock, 1986) describes studies of teachers' thought and decision making processes prior to and during instruction. These studies have used observations and self-reports to document the effects of expert teacher behavior in planning and decision making based on student achievement and attitudes. Tentative findings indicate that expert designers represent problems in an organized and accurate manner (Nelson, 1988). The findings from this body of research are contributing to a clarification of expertise related to instruction.

Nelson (1988) compared the design models and knowledge of expert and novice instructional designers and found that:

> Not surprisingly, differences between expert and novices mirrored the findings from previous expert/novice comparison studies in such domains as chess, electronics, and physics. That is, in comparison to novices, experts' knowledge structures are more highly organized and well-integrated, and experts are able to respond to and complete tasks more quickly and systematically. (p. 31)

Despite initial findings comparing expert and novice designers, only limited usable knowledge is currently available. Most studies investigate instructional design only in the context of the classroom. Obviously, many other studies of educators and trainers in varied settings are required to develop a clear understanding of expert and novice similarities and differences. Better control would be provided by a focus on the design of instructional materials without the confounding effects of classroom management.

Trainers and educators need instructional design expertise in order to plan, design, construct prototypes, and evaluate effective instruction. The effects of their efforts are dependent on the level of expertise they apply. The level of performance and expertise which is attained by their trainees and students is obviously influenced by the knowledge, skills, and attitudes of these instructors and the expertise that they have in designing instruction,

Expertise studies in instructional design processes imply a major issue in the application of AI to education and training endeavors. Can knowledge engineering and instructional design processes capture expertise and construct expert systems for the transfer of this expertise? Will educators and trainers, then, have ready access to the expertise needed to translate instructional decisions into specific instructional situations? M. David Merrill (1988) is attempting to capture the expertise required for effective instructional design using expert systems development tools. The complexity of this problem area and the difficulty of this task have been reported informally during national presentations to other instructional designers. Expertise research in the domain of instructional design still presents many unanswered questions such as: What are the areas of expertise required of an educator or a trainer? How can this expertise be transferred from expert to novice? Can this expertise be transferred to a computer and be readily available to novice users?

KNOWLEDGE ENGINEERING

Knowledge engineers acquire and utilize knowledge through a process of working intensively with domain experts in their area to determine how they make decisions and solve selected problems. The term "knowledge engineer" was coined by Edward Feigenbaum after the term "epistemological engineering" by Donald Miche. It came into frequent use with the terms "expert system" and "knowledge-based system" during the seventies. Knowledge engineering is a field which attempts to capture domain expertise and build knowledge-based systems such as expert systems and ICAI systems. Waterman (1986) describes knowledge engineering as a critical area of human endeavor:

> Over time, the knowledge engineering field will have an impact on all areas of human activity where knowledge provides the power for solving important problems. We can foresee two beneficial effects. The first and most obvious will be the development of knowledge systems that replicate and autonomously apply human expertise. For these systems, knowledge engineering will provide the technology for converting human knowledge into industrial power. The second benefit may be less obvious. As an inevitable side effect, knowledge engineering will catalyze a global effort to collect, codify, exchange, and exploit applicable forms of human knowledge. In this way, knowledge engineering will accelerate the development, clarification, and expansion of human knowledge itself. (p. vii-viii)

Knowledge engineering is a field of practice which was first viewed as an art or craft since it requires both creative abilities and interpersonal skills. Feigenbaum (1977) describes the practices in knowledge engineering as:

> . . . the art of bringing the principles and tools of AI research to bear on difficult application problems requiring experts' knowledge for their solution. The technical issues of acquiring this knowledge, representing it, and using it appropriately to construct and explain lines-of-reasoning, are important problems in the design of knowledge-based systems.

The analogies used to describe knowledge engineering reflect the combinations of art and applied science. For example, Buchanan and Shortcliffe (1984) use the analogy of knowledge engineering as mapping "an expert's knowledge into a program's knowledge base," whereas, Feigenbaum and McCorduck (1983) use the analogy of mining:

> The heuristic knowledge is hardest to get at because experts—or anyone else—rarely have the self-awareness to recognize what it is. So it must be mined out of their heads painstakingly, one jewel at a time. The miners are called *knowledge engineers.* Knowledge engineers, who study artificial intelligence, know how to represent knowledge in a computer. They know how to create reasoning programs to utilize knowledge. And they are interdisciplinary in spirit. Having mined these precious gems, they put together knowledge bases that form the most important part of expert systems. (p. 77)

According to Clancey (1987), the analogy of a model builder best defines the field:

> A knowledge engineer is an expert model builder, a kind of expert student. Proceeding with strong representational tools, he is a strikingly active student, constantly asking the expert questions, posing hypothetical scenarios, systematically analyzing how difficult problems and solutions are classified. (p. 247)

These definition and analogies of knowledge engineering allude to the complex art and science requirements for knowledge acquisition and knowledge utilization.

Knowledge Acquisition

Knowledge acquisition is the process of extracting, structuring, and organizing information from the domain expert and other sources (Waterman, 1986). This acquired knowledge may include procedures, strategies, and rules of thumb for problem solving. During the knowledge acquisition process, the expert is interviewed and questioned to determine how a selected problem is solved.

Knowledge acquisition begins by locating and collecting written sources of information such as manuals and references. Then, knowledge engineers may use a case study method to assist the domain expert in describing their problem solving and decision making processes. They observe and record in detail protocols which show how the expert solves the particular problem (Rauch-Hindin, 1988). During this process the knowledge engineer must become "somewhat of an expert in the problem domain" and the domain expert must become familiar with AI processes and tools (Waterman, 1986).

The human relationship skills required during the intensive interactions with the domain expert are frequently emphasized. For example, knowledge engineers require both listening and questioning skills:

> Clearly the knowledge engineers must be diplomats. In fact, several companies claim that for a knowledge engineer, people skills can be as important as technical skills. Knowledge engineers must be able to listen as well as ask, and to instill confidence in, and draw out, the expert regardless of personality differences. They must understand that because so much of the expert's knowledge is intuitive and subconscious, at times there is as much to be learned from rambling as from direct questions. (Rauch-Hindin, 1988, p. 107)

Knowledge acquistion is a complex process which has delayed the development of expert systems. Many knowledge engineers have described the knowledge acquisition process as the "bottleneck" of expert systems development (Feigenbaum & McCorduck, 1983). Consequently, AI research and development is presently seeking automated or semi-automated approaches to the transfer of expertise from domain expert to machines. Obviously, knowledge engineers will continue to be important forces in the acquistion and utilization of knowledge. Box 3.3 describes the potential impact of knowledge acquisition on education and training.

Box 3.3
Knowledge Acquisition in Education and Training

Educators and trainers are exposed to a vast and extensive knowledge base which they are expected to acquire and use. This exposure begins with preservice education and continues though on-the-job training, professional development, and work-based learning. Regardless of their efficiency and effectiveness as learners, given the enormity of the knowledge base, the vast majority of educators and trainers enter the initial phase of their careers at what knowledge engineers would deem to be novice status in the domain of instructional problem solving. The knowledge and expertise which they have for "on-demand" decision making in the instructional domain is relatively small compared to the vast amount to which they have been exposed and the extensive knowledge of expert instructors. In addition, the knowledge which novice instructors encounter is often a single instance of exposure with no opportunity to use the knowledge in an applied setting.

Many teacher education and instructional design training programs present their students with useful modes of instructional decision making which roughly parallel the scientific method. Further, these programs recommend general heuristics and preferred hierarchy criteria in instructional design and decision making. This hierarchy recommends the following levels of instructional decisions:

1. Instructional decisions related to objectives, assessment, media, time, corrections, and group management should first consider the knowledge that comes from research results directly relevant to the instructional problem or situation,

2. Next, consider research results which involve one step inferences where the instructional problem "almost matches" 75% or more of the situation,

3. If research does not exist (or is unknown to the instructional problem solver), use learning and instructional theories as the basis for most effective decision,

4. If learning and instructional theories fail to match the problem situation, then "best professional practices" and "rules of thumb" used by recognized instructional experts should be used, and

5. Finally, keep it simple and use "trial and error" strategies within the comfort zone of your instructional approach.

The knowledge acquisition and utilization capabilities required to effectively apply these general heuristics are obviously voluminous and complex from the perspective of the novice educator and trainer.

Can knowledge engineering procedures be effectively applied to these acquisition problems? Suppose knowledge acquisition were used to determine how instructional experts apply this hierarchy when confronted by a range of instructional problems. If this knowledge base could be captured, the resulting product could be stored through knowledge representation techniques in the computer's memory. This knowledge base could be accessed by requesting matches between the respective instructional problems of the novice and expert.

Given the current status of AI technologies, this illustration is more applicable to the planning and organization problems encountered by educators and trainers. It would be difficult to imagine how educators and trainers could consult with such a knowledge base amid the moment-by-moment responses of the student during guided discussions. However, the continuous use of the consulting system during instructional planning should gradually increase "on demand" expertise levels of the novice. With increasingly accessible knowledge bases available to novices, the plausibility of shortening the existing ten year knowledge acquisition requirement for experts seems highly likely.

Knowledge Utilization

Knowledge utilization is the process of establishing how knowledge will be used in problem solving. In order to effectively utilize the knowledge acquired from the domain expert and other sources, it must be represented in a form accessible to the computer and its user. In addition, an inference engine must be developed or selected to effectively utilize the knowledge. As described in the previous chapter, knowledge representation is a critical AI concept. Feigenbaum and McCorduck (1983) discuss knowledge representation questions that the knowledge engineer must solve:

> How shall the knowledge of a domain of work be represented as data structures in the memory of the computer in a manner in which they can be conveniently accessed for problem solving? (p. 79)

Knowledge utilization requires that this knowledge be effectively used in problem solving and decision making by the expert system and human users of that system. Designing an expert system consists of developing the rules and strategies for problem solving that are analyzed and programmed into the computer system. Knowledge engineers are responsible for clarifying steps in the problem solving process, developing prototypes, and maintaining knowledge-based systems. Competent knowledge engineers must know about AI processes and tools for the representation of knowledge.

Knowledge engineering may be defined broadly to include the general processes of knowledge acquisition and knowledge utilization or narrowly to focus on the expert systems development processes of planning, designing, constructing prototypes, and evaluating. The expert systems produced through knowledge engineering may be large computer-based consultants, ICAI modules, or job performance aids. The process, therefore, whether it results in a validated, usable consultant program or a teaching program, is a valuable enterprise for the developer. This process is like many research and development models in education and training. Knowledge engineering and expert system development processes are similar to other systems approaches such as computer programming and instructional design. Table 3.1 overviews the processes, computer languages, and tools used in knowledge engineering, instructional design, and software engineering (conventional computer programming.)

TABLE 3.1

Comparing Systems Approaches

for the Development of Computer Programs

Knowledge Engineering	Instructional Design	Software Engineering
Processes		
Expert Systems Development	Courseware Authoring	Computer Programming
Languages		
LISP Prolog	PILOT BASIC	Pascal FORTRAN
Tools		
Expert Systems Deveolopment Tools	Courseware Authoring Tools	Database Management Programs Spreadsheets
Products		
Expert Systems ITS Systems Intelligent Learning Environments	Drill and Practice Simulations CAI Tutorials	Databases Spreadsheets

EXPERT SYSTEMS DEVELOPMENT

Expert systems development is a systems approach which results in an expert system or an ICAI system as the product. This expert systems development process is described in numerous books and articles. Expert systems development processes are not limited to a specific set of stages, phases, or steps which are accepted for all domains of expertise (Waterman, 1986). Some writers prefer to discuss the stages or phases of knowledge engineering and others prefer to discuss the steps or tasks in the development of expert systems. At the present time, no consensus has emerged as to the best systematic approach to expert systems development.

An expert systems development process may be described in a four step cycle:

1. Plan,
2. Design,
3. Construct prototype, and
4. Evaluate.

A cycle of steps is proposed because the process of development is never complete—each step results in refinements which lead to revisions in the next step. This cyclical approach was selected because of its compatibility with instructional design processes, software engineering practices, and production systems development in general. The descriptions of each step have been synthesized from books by Rauch-Hindin (1988); Harmon, Maus, and Morrissey (1988); Waterman (1987); Harmon and King (1985); Hayes-Roth, Waterman, and Lenat (1983); and the *M.1 Manual of Teknowledge*, (1985).

The general steps of expert systems development are compatible with those in general systems approaches utilized by instructional designers. Although specific tasks may vary between knowledge engineering and instructional design because of product requirements, the general approaches are complementary. For example, a concurrent approach would be appropriate for the development of computer-based teaching systems such as ICAI systems. Figure 3. 1 shows the cycle of activities in expert systems development.

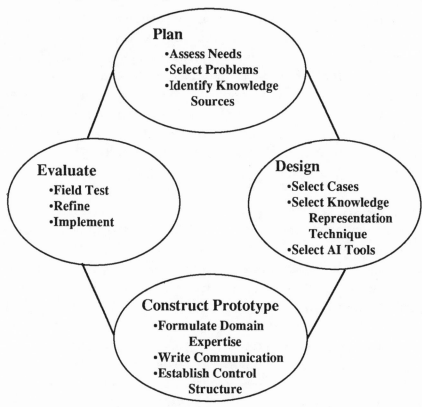

FIGURE 3.1 Expert Sytems Development Process

Plan

Planning is obviously a critical activity for most projects which involve a series of tasks. The general systems approach emphasizes planning as the first major step in the process of developing any product. Knowledge engineers and instructional designers each begin the process of product development with the planning step. The planning step in the repertoire of a knowledge engineer includes:

1. Assess needs,
2. Select problems, and
3. Identify knowledge sources.

Planning focuses on identification of the need, problem, scope, participants, purpose, and resources for the expert system project. Instructional designers use a similar repertoire to systematically plan instructional or training products. Written proposals are recommended during expert system development. Writing a project proposal improves planning and documentation. Maintaining a written plan or technical journal is critical to a systematic approach. These written plans will also be valuable resources for the development of documentation to accompany the computer program.

Assess Needs.   A prerequisite for any project is to determine need. Needs assessment identifies what is and what should be, and then prioritizes the revealed gaps (Kaufman, 1983). A need or problem must exist prior to committing the efforts of knowledge engineers and domain experts to the project. Knowledge engineers must determine needs through observation, interviews, or through the use of needs assessment instruments. Although some needs assessment instruments are available for general purposes, most instruments and surveys must be developed to match the purpose, goals, and objectives of each project. No general needs assessment instruments were found in the knowledge engineering literature.

Needs assessment is a familiar process to most educators and trainers who have responsibilities for the development of instructional or training products. Needs assessment is described in several books on instructional design as a process for determining whether an educational or training need exists (Rodriguez, 1988; Kaufman, 1982).

Only some needs can be met through the development of expert systems. For example, expert systems might be selected to meet the needs for decision making during a training problem involving electrical troubleshooting, but might be inappropriate for solving a specific workplace problem involving relationships among specific individuals. Problem selection should be based upon needs assessment and the appropriateness of expert system development for the identified need.

Select Problems. A systematic approach should be used in clarifying and selecting problems during the cycle of expert systems development. Problem solving requires that the knowledge engineer determine whether the expert systems development process or expert systems products will meet the needs identified during needs assessment. Obviously, a significant need must exist or the effort to develop an expert system should not be made. Unfortunately, many problems cannot be solved through the use of expert systems. Identifying the problem and determining its scope is a difficult task for knowledge engineers (Waterman, 1986). Novice knowledge engineers must acquire experience working with experienced knowledge engineers regarding the feasibility of effective expert systems related to identified problems. The problems initially considered by the knowledge engineer are often too broad and must be narrowed for successful development. A major concern during problem selection is whether the knowledge-based system will be able to perform competently in the role of a consultant or teaching system. If, during the planning step the knowledge engineer determines that these problems cannot be solved by a knowledge-based system, then each inappropriate problem should be narrowed or referred to another type of developer.

Problem selection in expert systems development involves choosing a domain and a task for knowledge clarification. Knowledge engineers are more likely to be successful if they initially select limited tasks in domains where the structures and procedures of expertise are known. A *domain* is the area of application, or collection of knowledge, which comprises the desired expertise. For example, special education laws is a domain within education that involves a collection of knowledge and expertise. The *task* is to define a limited problem within the domain which represents a subarea of the domain. For example, the classification of learning disabled students is a subdomain within special education law and a task requiring both knowledge and decision making. A *case* is a specific problem or situation which requires task performance. For example, a case might involve determining whether Johnny is a learning disabled student when specific information about his background and assessment results are given. To be an effective area for knowledge engineering, the domain and task must be limited and understood by experts (Teknowledge, Inc., 1985). Education and training offer many domains where expertise presently exists and the scope of the problem allows expert systems development. However, many of the domains and tasks in education and training have not been adequately clarified and documented for expertise to be transferred.

Several criteria have been suggested for determining appropriate domains and tasks for expert systems development. Table 3.2 provides a brief checklist to determine whether a problem can plausibly be selected for expert systems development.

TABLE 3.2
Problem Selection Criteria

	Yes	No	Unsure
Can a domain expert perform the task competently?			
Does the task require knowledge and expertise?			
Are facts available to the system user?			
Are facts stable during the consultation?			
Can all solutions be listed?			
Are important objects and behaviors in the domain observable?			

ADDITIONAL CRITERIA
FOR SIMPLE OR FIRST EXPERT SYSTEM

	Yes	No	Unsure
Can the problem be solved over a telephone?			
Can the problem be solved in less than ten minutes?			

Identify Knowledge Sources. The project proposal should list and describe sources of knowledge for the project. During planning, needed sources of knowledge or expertise should be located. Compiled sources of knowledge are books, reports, checklists, or manuals. Most expert systems obtain knowledge and information from live experts who are competent in solving the identified domain and task performance. Unfortunately, the time of experts is very valuable and therefore may be difficult to capture. Most projects require at least one expert who is competent to solve the problem or to complete many tasks effectively in the domain of interest. Although major projects usually involve more than one expert, procedures must be established for determining which expertise will dominate when experts disagree. Multiple expert problems and advantages and limitations of expert systems based upon more than one expert are described in articles on expert systems development.

Planning for the instructional designer is similar to that of the knowledge engineer. However, the products of instructional design, by definition, have a focus on teaching, not consulting. Expert instructional designers explore numerous options during the planning step. Some of these options involve the use of computers as a delivery tool. If during the planning step other media prove more useful, then the instructional designer will not pursue development of a computer-based product.

Instructional design models sometimes label the processes of determining goals and selecting problems as needs assessment and identifying knowledge sources as resource identification. Obviously, these activities are compatible with activities undertaken by the knowledge engineer. Needs analysis determines the goals for the project and analyzes the information gathered during the needs assessment process. Both instructional designers and knowledge engineers must be sure to clarify the problem areas and select appropriate goals for the projects. Needs analysis models such as the Organizational Elements Model of Kaufman (1982) are comprehensive approaches to planning which are an integral part of the instructional design process and are quite compatible with knowledge engineering processes in the development of expert systems.

Design

Design requires acquiring and clarifying knowledge about the problem solving domain prior to prototype construction on a computer. During the design process, the knowledge engineer must learn about problem solving in the domain under scrutiny. The design step in the cycle of expert systems development includes the following activities:

1. Select cases,
2. Select knowledge representation technique, and
3. Select AI tools.

The design process attempts to acquire, understand, and organize the knowledge from appropriate sources into accessible structures of expertise. Knowledge engineering and instructional design require similar types of activities in the design step.

Knowledge engineers spend considerable time and effort at the beginning of a project and throughout the development cycle, seeking knowledge which is explicit and accessible (Waterman, 1986). Large amounts of knowledge from compiled sources such as books or articles may be useless to knowledge engineers as they attempt to clarify the knowledge and expertise used by competent problem solvers. However, some knowledge and information must be acquired from these compiled sources, and knowledge engineers usually need to immerse themselves in these sources to acquire core concept and critical information and to enhance productivity of their interactions with experts.

When knowledge engineers begin the clarification process of structuring and organizing knowledge they must consider what concepts and relationships are required to describe problem solving processes in a given domain (Waterman, 1986). Strategies and subtasks must also be identified and described. Unfortunately, AI research has already shown that experts do not understand their own unconscious problem solving processes. Discovering the knowledge used by experts or competent problem solvers is an exciting pursuit of knowledge engineers which is not yet fully understood. This exploration has been described in numerous books and articles as an art, not a science. Fortunately for educators and trainers, this process has many similarities to the observation, questioning, and design skills required of an effective teacher or trainer. Instructional designers should clarify the goals, objectives, and content during the design step, and the successes and failures of knowledge engineers may enhance their abilities to do so.

Select Cases. The selection of a set of cases or specific problems to be solved will greatly facilitate understanding the knowledge used by the competent problem solver. Most approaches to knowledge engineering recommend asking the expert to discuss the solution to a specific problem or case. As experts begin to discuss the solutions to a range of problems or cases, similarities can be identified in the knowledge required for solution. In addition, differences between problems or cases in the set yield important guidelines for clarifying knowledge. Obviously, educators and trainers have been aware of the importance of similarities and differences or examples and non-examples in developing a student's understanding of concepts for quite some time (Gagne, 1985; Merrill & Tennyson, 1977; Engelmann & Carnine, 1982). Establishing a range of cases or examples from simple to complex is a useful instructional design step (Ferrara, Prater, & Baer, 1987).

Select Knowledge Representation Technique. Knowledge representation techniques must be selected to allow adequate storage of knowledge and information. In the ideal situation, the knowledge engineer will select the appropriate knowledge representation technique based upon the type of knowledge acquired from the sources used by the expert. For example, if the expert operates with a large number of rules, then rules will be the primary knowledge representation technique. However, if the expert uses maps extensively in domain decision making, then direct or analogical representation would be more appropriate. At present, knowledge engineers have been limited in the knowledge representation techniques because most microcomputers have only rule-based representation techniques available. Some frame and graphic representational systems are currently being used for research purposes in the development of expert systems.

Select AI Tools. The selection of AI tools or the expert systems development tool is an important task which is unfortunately limited in educational and training settings. For any given project a number of tools may be adequate. Most existing expert systems were constructed with tools chosen because of their familiarity to the developer, or their capability to run on a developer's hardware. Factors in the proper consideration of expert systems development tools and hardware are discussed later in this chapter.

Instructional designers use a design process similar to knowledge engineering. In the development of computer-assisted instruction materials, the instructional designer will work with subject matter area experts to clarify the content. Computer-assisted instruction programs can be developed on authoring tools or by using traditional programming languages. The shortcomings of AI researchers in selecting appropriate problems represents a fruitful area where education and training can advance AI methodologies.

Construct Prototype

A prototype is a program that demonstrates the capabilities of the knowledge-based system in solving problems. Developers should construct a small prototype early in the expert systems development process. Knowledge engineers will gain knowledge about the concepts and relationships in the knowledge-based system from this initial implementation. Prototype development involves encoding the knowledge into an expert systems development tool or AI language so that the expert may begin to see how the computer will interact with the user. For example, a rule-based tool will require the knowledge engineer to enter rules used by the expert to solve specific cases into the knowledge base. If prototype development is successful, the case will be solved successfully when the expert system is run. If the expert system fails to solve the case, then further rules may be added or rules may be changed to improve the system's performance. Prototype construction is a step in knowledge engineering that is more difficult to implement in systems approaches such as software engineering and instructional design. A working prototype is difficult to achieve with traditional programming tools. Some instructional designers indicate that one major advantage of authoring systems for CAI development is the potential for prototyping. Techniques such as storyboarding have been used by instructional designers as a variation on prototype construction. The following activities are undertaken during the construction of a prototype:

1. Formulate domain expertise,
2. Write communication, and
3. Establish control structures.

A demonstration prototype is initially developed to handle some typical problems or cases encountered by a competent problem solver or expert. This prototype program is used to test ideas about the problem, scope, and knowledge representation technique to be used in the expert system. This demonstration prototype might contain approximately 50 rules and perform adequately on a small set of test cases or problems (Waterman, 1986). Field test prototypes are revised through testing on a larger set of test cases or problems and may involve 100 rules or more. A commercial or production prototype should exhibit high quality and reliable performance in a real-world environment. Although a prototype with these characteristics requires maintenance, it should be considered a useful expert system.

Formulate Domain Expertise. Knowledge and information from the domain expert must be formulated in such a manner as to be stored in the computer program. Prototype construction requires the formulation of goals and rules in the most commonly used expert systems development tools available on microcomputers. Frame-based development systems and object-oriented programming are now available to educators and trainers as tools for prototype construction. The developer must represent the knowledge of the domain expert in the form which leads to best accessibility and efficiency.

Write Communication. If the prototype expert system is to communicate effectively with the user, clear questions and explanations must be written by the knowledge engineer and the domain expert. Questions must be written to gather information and facts about the case from the user. In addition, explanations or displays must be written to communciate effectively with users when they request additional information. These questions and displays may be continuously refined during prototype construction to clarify the communication. Further information on explanatory capabilities is provided in Chapter Four.

Establishing Control Structures. The control of the interactions is determined by the expert systems development tools and the inference engine as described in the previous chapter. However, changing the sequence of interactions or improving the ease of use may require a modification in the control structures. AI languages and most expert systems development tools contain procedures for modifying control to improve the prototype.

Evaluate

The evaluation process is common to all areas of science and technology. *Evaluation* is a process for continuous revision of a product during the cycles of development. How does the evaluation of expert systems differ from general evaluation processes? The evaluation step in the cycle of expert systems development includes the following activities:
1. Field testing,
2. Refinement, and
3. Implementation.

Most books and articles on expert systems development describe a process of product revision and testing which is similar to the product evaluation cycle of instructional design. However, AI has not adopted the sophisticated evaluation cycles of formative and summative evaluation common to educators and trainers.

Evaluation is the process used to improve the product during development and to judge and test performance by the final product. This evaluation process is highly recommended for the development of expert systems, decision support systems, and intelligent computer-assisted instruction systems. According to Parry (1986):

... expert systems evolve through a continuous interactive process of design, development, and evaluation. (p. 16)

Although AI developers and knowledge engineers indicate the importance of field testing and validation, few AI research products have been tested using demanding evaluation procedures. One notable exception was the testing of the MYCIN program near the completion of the ten year project (Buchanan & Shortliffe, 1984). Although MYCIN is not presently used in a real world setting, the evaluation and validation procedures were systematically applied in a manner similar to those used by the expert instructional designers. Evaluation is a term that is familiar to educators and trainers.

Field test. Field testing activities in expert systems development are complicated by the fact that there may be no formal way to prove an answer is the correct or best solution. User acceptance is a critical component of evaluation. If an expert system is unfriendly, confusing, tedious, or frustrating, then it will be unacceptable to users regardless of performance results (Waterman, 1986). Factors which might be considered in field testing include utility, flexibility, ease of use, intelligibility of output, speed, efficiency, and reliability (Parry, 1986).

Prototypes should be carefully field tested to determine needed changes. Field testing is simply executing cases or problems which were selected during the design process. Both typical and unusual cases should be run to identify the strengths and weaknesses of the expert system. A review of cases or problems by experts will assure the knowledge engineers that the expert system is responding to an appropriate range of problems in similar fashion to experts' response patterns. Blind reviews in which the best domain experts compare solutions obtained by the machine and human generated solutions without knowledge of machine involvement are highly recommended for final field tests (Parry, 1986).

Refine. Several groups benefit from the continuous refinement of an expert system. Knowledge engineers depend upon evaluation for testing and improving their knowledge bases and the functioning of their knowledge-based systems. Domain experts must assess how their knowledge is being used in the program. Evaluation promotes communication between the knowledge engineer and the domain expert.

More knowledge is added to the expert system through the continuing process of redesign and prototype revision. Several different prototypes will be created during the usual course of expert systems development. Then final revisions may be made prior to implementation in the real-world setting.

Implement. Real-world settings demand ease of use and smooth execution. Many useful technologies have failed because of problems encountered in proving their usefulness when they are moved into real-world settings. Expert systems development processes and AI products must continue to demonstrate utility in research laboratories, and additionally, in classrooms and training centers. AI products must be non-obtrusive and not significantly disruptive of the day-to-day routines of educators and trainers to prove their usefulness.

During the implementation of any new technology, leadership is needed from management and policy making levels for successful transfer. Leaders need to be assured that the new technology will result in organizational and productivity improvement at an acceptable level of risk. Change for change sake is not important to effective leaders; change has associated costs and risks as well as potential benefits. The goals of the organization are more important than the new technology. To be successful, AI technologies and expert systems will need to improve and contribute to the goals of the organization or needed leadership will not be forthcoming from management and policy making levels. Leaders must consider the benefits and risks involved in expert system technology, identify barriers to its use, establish strategies to overcome them, and attend to the details in the organization to ensure successful technology transfer.

Orientation and information are needed to overcome resistance to the new technology. Education and training of all individuals involved in the new technology will result in a higher success rate for technology transfer. Leaders must see that individuals in the organization are familiar with the terminology used in discussing the new technology. In addition, individuals in the organization must be trained to use the technology effectively in their own jobs or to understand how its use by others will impact their areas of responsibility. Initial use of the technology may result in a short-term loss in productivity which can be minimized by effective adaptation and training strategies. Support must be provided until productivity gains are visible. When the new technology contributes to productivity, individuals in the organization will be more likely to continue using the technology and to seek ways to expand its impact. Organizational commitment exemplified in leadership behavior is required if individuals are to begin, continue, and expand uses for unfamiliar technology.

These postulates of successful technology transfer are no different for AI applications than for any new technology. However, the culture which fosters AI science and technology seems particularly alien to the education and training cultures. The perceived "gap" is sufficiently large to require more careful attention to the postulates than would be necessary for successful transfer from a less alien culture.

Maintenance is a critical factor in the continuing success of innovative computer technologies. Maintenance requires the continuing correction of errors and the continued improvements to meet the needs of users. According to Carrico, Girard, and Jones (1989):

> Maintenance must not be ignored. Software maintenance is the process of modifying existing operational software while leaving its primary functions intact. (p. 219)

Maintenance demands a commitment of time, money, and resources. All software needs maintenance if successful implementation is to continue.

AI TOOLS

AI Hardware

Expert systems and expert systems development tools run on a wide range of computers including microcomputers, workstations, LISP machines, and mainframes. The varying cost and sophistication of these computers requires that educators and trainers evaluate products carefully before selection. Expert systems development tools and AI languages each have different hardware requirements. Some AI tools and languages only run on specific types of computers. Some tools and languages require expanded memories or graphic capabilities. Overall, AI hardware may be divided into four general categories:

1. Mainframe or minicomputers.
2. Conventional workstations, mostly UNIX-based systems.
3. LISP machines or workstations designed to run the LISP language.
4. Microcomputers such as DOS machines and Macintosh.

Mainframe and minicomputers are used in corporations and universities to run computer networks. Some expert systems development tools have recently been developed to run on these computers because of commercial demand. Unfortunately, these computers have poor graphic environments at present which limit their usefulness in AI. AI languages such as LISP and Prolog have become available for mainframes and minicomputers.

Conventional workstations can be used for applications in engineering and science as well as for AI research. Many hybrid expert system development tools are available for these workstations. Appropriate AI languages and object oriented programming environments are also available. The costs of workstations may be prohibitive for education and training uses in some settings although costs are decreasing at a regular annual rate.

LISP machines are computers which have been developed specifically to handle the LISP language and provide an AI programming environment. LISP machines are primarily used at AI research and development laboratories and major universities. Harmon, Maus, and

Morrissy (1988) report that 85 percent of U.S. sales of AI and expert systems products have been to universities, the military, and aerospace companies. LISP machines purchases have been confined to research and prototype development environments. These machines are extremely expensive and until recently have been limited in their abilities to run other applications.

During recent years, a large number of expert systems development tools have become available for microcomputers. Although microcomputers have less memory, processing power, and graphic capability than LISP machines, the low cost of microcomputers and their accessibility makes then them most likely environment for the development of expert systems in education and training. Dramatic improvements are being made in the memory, processing power, and graphic capabilities of microcomputers each year. For example, Apple Computer and Texas Instrument have joined efforts to release the microExplorer, an AI workstation which has many of the capabilities of the LISP machine at the cost of a high end microcomputer.

AI Languages

The numerous programming languages used for AI research and expert systems development are valuable tools. These programming languages are translators from particular machine languages to a higher-level language which is easier for the researcher and developer to use. Learning a new language requires time and effort. AI research has required knowledge of a symbolic processing language such as LISP or Prolog. These languages are significantly different from algorithmic languages such as FORTRAN, Pascal, C, or BASIC.

All computer programming languages provide methods for specifying the objects and procedures needed to solve specific problems. Some programming languages have been developed in fields like science, business, and education to make the specification easier in that field. For example, courseware authoring languages such as PILOT were developed to reduce the level of complexity involved in producing instruction on computers. Researchers in AI have

developed programming languages which make both general problem solving and the development of expert systems easier.   In
addition, these programming languages usually provide an environment for writing, modifying, and debugging programs (Barr &
Feigenbaum, 1982).

AI languages and environments provide the programmer with the
capabilities of manipulating arbitrary symbols.   The emphasis on
manipulating symbols and defining functions has differentiated AI
languages from programming languages which are dependent upon
numeric and algorithmic features.   AI languages and environments
are valuable tools for research and for developing AI programs and
expert systems.

LISP.   LISP is the second oldest programming language in widespread usage (FORTRAN is oldest).   As previously indicated, the
name LISP is derived from the words "list processing."   LISP was in-
vented in 1958 by John McCarthy, an AI founder.   Although expert
systems development tools may soon change this perception, at
present, most individuals would not consider themselves AI scientists
or knowledge engineers unless they could demonstrate competence in
LISP by developing interesting prototypes.   LISP is now in the
process of becoming "standardized" with the widespread acceptance
of Common LISP as a language and programming environment.

Although a description of LISP programming procedures is
beyond the scope of this book, the following are key ideas of LISP
computation adapted from McCarthy (1978):
1. Computes with arbitrary symbolic expressions,
2. Creates lists through associations of primitives called atoms,
3. Links lists at different levels,
4. Controls structure by creating functions from simpler
   functions, and
5. Uses an evaluation function as an interpreter.
LISP is the AI programming language which is used most extensively
in the United States.

Prolog. The symbolic processing language, Prolog, is becoming popular throughout the world. Prolog is the AI language chosen by the Japanese for the Fifth Generation Project as well as the AI language of choice in Europe. The name Prolog comes from the idea of "programming in logic." Prolog is characterized as a descriptive and declarative language. Programming in Prolog requires that the relationships between objects in the problem be described. In addition, to solve the problem, facts about the objects and their relationships must be declared. The Prolog approach to programming is to describe known objects and relationships about a problem, and to declare what facts and relationships are "true" about the potential solutions. According to Clocksin and Mellish (1984) in their classic book *Programming in Prolog* :

> When a computer is programmed in Prolog, the actual way the computer carries out the computation is specified partly by the logical declarative semantics of Prolog, partly by what new facts Prolog can "infer" from the given ones, and only partly by explicit control information supplied by the programmer. (p. viii)

Prolog may be used in applications such as databases, mathematical logic, understanding natural language, symbolic equation solving, abstract problem solving, and other areas of AI research.

Object Oriented Programming. Several AI languages and programming environments involve the decription and manipulation of objects. These programming languages are called object orient programming languages or environments. SMALLTALK, developed by Alan Kay at the Xerox Palo Alto Research Center, was one of the first object-oriented programming languages. At present many other object oriented programming languages and environments are being used to develop AI and commercial applications. Some versions of LISP and Logo now include the capabilities to program objects. The Macintosh Computer and its interface system uses object oriented programming concepts. HYPERCARD and its language HYPER-TALK are a recent object oriented programming environment and language.

Expert Systems Development Tools

Expert systems development tools are computer programs which are commercially available to individuals who want to develop expert systems to solve specific problems in their settings. These tools or "shells" are constrained high level programming environments which are designed to assist with product development (Harmon, Maus, and Morrissey,1988). Some expert systems development tools are as easy to use as an electronic spreadsheet or database management system. Other tools require weeks or months to master much like a programming language (Hofmeister & Ferrara, 1986). Different tools allow different approaches to the way knowledge is represented. Expert systems development tools which facilitate the use of rules, induction, and frames are readily available. Effective tools save the developer time and effort by providing an interface, inference engine, and knowledge-based editing features which would otherwise have to be developed.

Many tools are becoming commercially available for the development of expert systems. These tools will be useful for educators and trainers who want to develop decision support systems, expert systems, or knowledge system modules to interact with other applications. A review of these tools is provided in books by Rauch-Hindin (1988); Harmon, Maus, and Morrissey (1988); and Waterman (1987) and monthly newsletters such as *Expert Systems Strategies*. Since these expert systems development tools are constantly improving and changing, they will not be reviewed here.

Most microcomputer-based expert systems development tools represent knowledge in an easy-to-use IF-THEN production system format with backward chaining and some limited forward chaining capabilities. Some object oriented development environments have become available for microcomputers. The accessibility and low cost of expert systems development tools creates the opportunity for a unique type of teaching strategie which allows novices to develop small expert systems. Box 3.4 describes the processes of novice knowledge engineering as a new instructional tool.

Box 3.4

Novice Knowledge Engineering

A creative use of expert systems development tools in education and training is called "novice knowledge engineering" (Lippert, 1989). *Novice knowledge engineering* is a teaching strategy which requires the students or novices to construct a knowledge base and develop a small expert system to demonstrate their problem solving competencies in the domain of study. In order to construct a small expert system, the novice must complete all the stages of the expert systems development process. By requiring the novice to "teach" the naive computer, this process forces the student to gain a clear understanding of the knowledge and skills necessary to solve the specific problem. According to Lippert (1989):

> . . . it has often been said that the best way to learn is to teach. In this regard, the similarity between instructional design and knowledge engineering is worth mentioning, because students commented that they felt they were in effect planning instruction when they selected and sequenced the content, and decide how to make various relationships within the content explicit. (p. 17)

Novice knowledge engineering has demonstrated promise in a limited number of exploratory studies. For example, Trollip and Lippert (1987) report success with this process while teaching the factors of screen design to instructional design students:

> . . . the construction of knowledge bases acts as a tool or probe to explore the acquistion, organization and utilization of knowledge by individual students. (p. 47)

A series of initial studies in the use of this process in engineering courses were described by Starfield, Butala, England, and Smith (1983). Recent studies have explored novice knowledge engineering process with younger students in biology classes (Wideman and Owston, 1988).

CHAPTER SUMMARY

• The study of expertise lends insight into the processes of expert problem solvers. Expertise is the body of knowledge and information which underlies the ability to solve difficult problems and make decisions. Domain experts achieved their expertise through study, practice, and experience. Clarification of the specific knowledge and reasoning underlying domain expertise enables this knowledge and information to be captured in knowledge bases. The transfer of this knowledge and expertise can be provided through computer-based consultation and teaching.

• Knowledge engineering is a field of AI practice which focuses on knowledge acquisition and utilization. Knowledge aquisition is a complex process of extracting, structuring, and organizing knowledge from domain experts and other sources. Knowledge utilization is the complementary process of determining how this knowledge will be used in problem solving and decision making by either humans or machines.

• Expert systems development is a systems approach which results in an expert system or ICAI system as a product. The expert system process may be viewed as a four step cycle that includes planning, designing, constructing prototypes, and evaluating the product.

• Plan is the first critical activity for most projects. Planning requires needs assessment, problem selection, and the identification of knowledge sources. During the plan step, the need, problem, scope, participants, purpose, and resources for the expert systems project are clarified.

• Design involves the selection of the set of problem situations to be solved, and the choice of knowledge representation techniques and AI tools. Knowledge engineers study compiled sources and meet with experts to discover the structure and organization of knowledge within the domain.

• Prototype construction is a process of goal and knowledge clarification, writing of questions and explanations that communicate with the user, and establishment of control structures. A prototype demonstrates the capabilities of the expert system during early development and continuous refinement.

• Continuous evaluation and refinement through field testing during implementation will result in a useful product. The evaluation process is used to improve the product during development and test performance by the final product. Field testing activities determine needed changes in the expert systems product. Implementation requires leadership and maintenance procedures if technology transfer is to be successful.

• AI tools run on a range of computers that encompass mainframes, workstations, LISP machines, and personal microcomputers. AI products may be developed in either AI languages or by using special expert systems development tools. Numerous programming languages such as LISP and Prolog, and object oriented programming environments such as SMALLTALK are used in AI research.

• Expert systems development tools allow individuals without extensive training in knowledege engineering to develop expert systems. Many expert systems development tools are becoming commerically available at low costs for microcomputers.

SCORECARD				
Will AI Research and Development Efforts Contribute to Education and Training?				
Topics	Question Dimensions			
	Feasibility	Improved Effectiveness	Capacity Enhancing	Future Utility
Transfer of Expertise				
Knowledge Engineering				
Knowledge Acquisition				
Knowledge Utilization				
Expert Systems Development Process				
AI Hardware				
AI Languages				
Expert Systems Development Tools				

Comments:

DIRECTIONS

Imagine a time in the future when there will be a unique type of non-fiction "writer." Instead of writing on paper, individuals choose to clarify and communicate expertise through "writing" knowledge and information into a computer's knowledge base. These "knowledge engineers" develop their projects by determining whose knowledge and expertise will be captured. Then, the selected domain experts spend extensive time periods with the knowledge engineer, who poses cases and situations, provides problems, and asks questions of them to capture all aspects of their knowledge. The knowledge engineers design, construct, and revise prototypes of that knowledge using sophisticated expert system development tools. Finally, the expert system is ready to consult and communicate the knowledge of the experts to anyone who has access to the computer program representing this knowledge and expertise.

Few educators and trainers doubt the value of acquiring and utilizing knowledge. What is less clear is whether the processes of knowledge engineering will contribute to effectiveness in this acquisition and utilization. Knowledge engineering has been proposed as a process of knowledge acquisition and knowledge utilization. As an emergent field of research and development, the exact meaning and applications of these components are unclear.

Educators and trainers need specific expertise in many areas of work productivity. To be productive, the work of teaching, delivering and managing instruction, developing and collecting materials, assessing and improving learner productivity, evaluation, and research must be performed with the appropriate knowledge and skills. We propose that the knowledge engineering processes are likely to improve the productivity of educators and trainers in the future.

Of what value is the clarification of expertise? Educators and trainers have always demonstrated an interest in analyzing expertise in the form of skills. AI processes and tools will complement instructional design approaches for them by enhancing the results of knowledge analysis. Specific knowledge is needed to guide and inform the decision making of educators and trainers. Effective educators and trainers have acquired expertise which novices need to have and use if they are to be effective.

Examining the purposes and practices of knowledge engineering may hold promise for educators and trainers. For example, if the object of instruction is conceptualized as "the transfer of expertise," would we conceive the instructional process differently? Wouldn't that concept expand the instructional focus from the assignment and task completion level to the development of generalizable problem solving strategies? Would it also emphasize the interrelationships and dependencies among learning outcomes in different domains and focus trainers' and educators' efforts upon the integration of information, attitudes, cognitive strategies, and skills? Would it reinforce the instructional purposes of evaluating student outcomes as being equal to or greater in importance than the institutional purpose of assigning grades or determining promotion to some next level? Thinking about instruction as transfer of expertise would promote examination of the assumptions, practices, and accepted wisdom underlying current best practices. Advances in the technologies of instruction are often the result of different ideas or a different frame of reference than has been previously used; therefore the examination of instruction from the knowledge engineering perspective could well lead to improved technologies emerging in training and education.

The processes of clarifying problems and listing alternative solutions are useful even without computer application. Knowledge acquisition through the knowledge engineering process is a useful activity which makes heuristic knowledge explicitly clear and easily accessible. This clarification process can be used by educators and trainers to identify what they know and do not know during problem analysis. As the knowledge engineer proceeds to organize and analyze the existing expertise within a domain, a subtle benefit occurs in that existing knowledge and information acquires greater clarity. Partial gaps in knowledge become better defined, and empty spaces in the knowledge domain become hauntingly obvious. This knowledge utilization process accelerates and facilitates representation in a knowledge base which promotes more effective transfer of expertise and knowledge utilization.

Will AI tools assist educators and trainers in acquiring and utilizing expertise? Tools often become merely toys if not effectively utilized. Like presents after a birthday party, the new tools of education and training frequently end up on a shelf. If we acquire these computer-based tools, will they become dust collectors after their novelty wears off, or will they become invaluable aids? We have been and will continue to be cautiously optimistic about the likely effects of AI hardware and expert systems development tools upon educators and trainers. We have made the argument that commonalities among ends is more than sufficient to overcome the perceived differences involving "alien" culture's means. Educators and trainers, at the same time, must confront the myth and reality of their reluctance to systematically employ available technologies in everyday practices in their field of endeavor. The level of technological complexity represented by AI hardware and expert systems development tool configurations is certainly more challenging (and more exciting) than colored chalk, super-8-film cartridges, overhead transparencies, and tape/slide presentation technologies. By way of contrast, utilization of the listed audio-visual technologies has not always characterized education and training efforts where such use would be most appropriate. Delving into AI hardware and expert systems development tools involves a much higher level of risk and effort for the trainer or educator than does technology such as super-8; yet we judge it more likely to be undertaken (and more worthwhile for having been undertaken) because the plausible outcomes are much more desirable and hold the promise of much greater effects than does a less complex technology. Educators and trainers may have overused the "absence of sufficient resources" rationale in the past for not adapting any given technology to their pursuits; however, the proposed relative advantage to be gained in those situations does not begin to approach the plausible impact represented in AI hardware (in microcomputer format) and expert systems development tools when they are taken to task by educators and trainers.

The expert systems development process is compatible with previous systems approaches in education and training such as instructional design and applied behavior analysis. The process and tools of knowledge engineering will be useful in future work related to clarifying concepts, tasks, and decision making. The intellectual power of the expert systems development process is an arresting consideration for educators and trainers. The very idea of teaching a computer to embody expertise that has been acquired across 10-12 years of demanding work in demanding performance environments, to further represent that expertise in ways that can be understood and accessed by novices, and to hint that application of the captured expertise can substantially improve human performance across many domains of knowledge has obvious significance. In the history of education and training, many individuals have been recognized, even lionized, for the expertise they acquired and used in research, development, and application. Each educator and trainer has a list of personal favorites and likely fantasizes about bringing them together to asist in particularly challenging instructional problem solving situations. A consulting staff of (make your own list) would represent the kind of inellectual power all educators and trainers would like to have at their beck and call.

Having easy, problem indexed access to such expertise would have been unthinkable in the first four decades of this century. Imagine the reaction to the proposition having been made in 1942 (World War II aside) that a first year teacher could readily access and use the expertise of such experts. Yet, AI research has provided a very real means to access the incredibly vast and complex domains of expertise as an everyday practice.

Given the existence of this capability, we propose that joining knowledge engineering processes with the strong reality orientation existent in education and training environments holds great promise for improved conception about and use of expertise in the development of effective instruction. Such a venture could be established in the contexts of expert systems development or instructional design processes, or in both. A joint effort, it seems, would be much more likely to result in realizing the use of this powerful capability than would separate efforts by experts in either field.

This strategy seems wise in that the success of such an expert system depends upon its extant capability to permeate day-to-day operation in the workplace by being a convenient tool for completing the tasks of real, daily work. The reality orientation and instructional design context provide the necessary, but not necessarily sufficient, characteristics for such permeating effect to occur. At the same time, knowledge engineering and expert systems processes enable us to develop the heuristics to be contained in the system, and structure chunks of expertise which correspond to specific characteristics of instructional settings and problems. With the challenges we face, education and training need to seek powerful technologies equal to the ever changing demands they currently face and the more complex demands that are certain to emerge in our future. While developing such a system may require an effort level as high as 35 person years, the investment will be recouped many times over in a very short interval with the expert system's widespread use.

TOPICAL REFERENCES

Transfer of Expertise

Fischler, M.A., & Firschein, O. (1987). *Intelligence: The eye, the brain, and the computer.* Reading, MA: Addison-Wesley Publishing.

Clancey, W.J. (1987). *Knowledge-based tutoring—The GUIDON program.* Cambridge, MA: The MIT Press.

Knowledge Engineering

Carrico, M.A., Girard, J.E., & Jones, J.P. (1989). *Building knowledge systems–Developing and managing rule-based applications.* New York: Intertext–McGraw-Hill.

Hayes-Roth, F., Waterman, D.A., & Lenat, D.B. (1983). *Building expert systems.* Reading, MA: Addison-Wesley Publishing.

Harmon, P., & King, D. (1985). *Expert systems—Artificial intelligence in business.* New York: John Wiley & Sons.

Harmon, P., Maus, R., & Morrissey, W. (1988). *Expert systems tools and applications.* New York: John Wiley & Sons.

Waterman, DA. (1986). *A guide to expert systems.* Reading, MA: Addison-Wesley Publishing.

Weiss, S.M. (1984). *A practical guide to designing expert systems.* Totowa, NJ: Rowman & Allanheld.

AI Tools

Harmon, P., Maus, R., & Morrissey, W. (1988). *Expert systems tools and applications*. New York: John Wiley & Sons.

Hayes-Roth, F., Waterman, D.A., & Lenat, D.B. (1983). *Building expert systems*. Reading, MA: Addison-Wesley Publishing.

Rauch-Hindin, W.B. (1988). *A guide to commercial artificial intelligence*. Englewood Cliffs, NJ: Prentice Hall.

AI Languages

Clocksin, W.F., & Mellish, C.S. (1984). *Programming in Prolog*. New York: Springer-Verlag.

Shafer, D. (1986). *Artificial intelligence programming on the Macintosh*. Indianapolis, IN: Howard W. Sams & Co.

Touretzky, D.S. (1984). *LISP—A gentle introduction to symbolic computation*. New York: Harper & Row, Publishers.

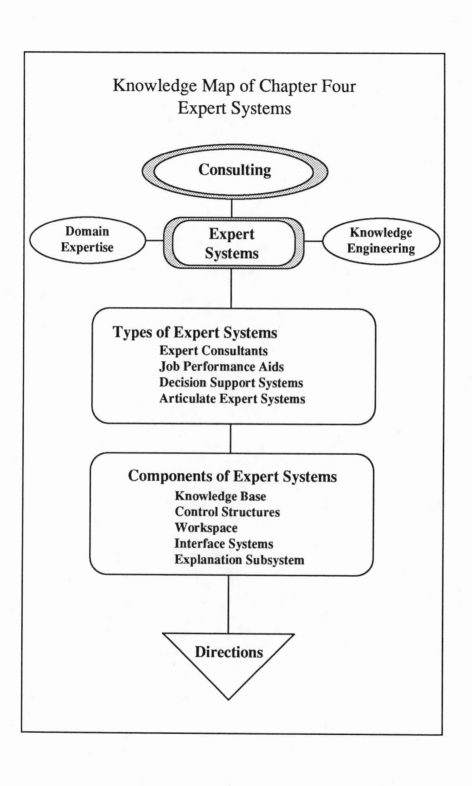

Knowledge Map of Chapter Four
Expert Systems

Consulting

Domain
Expertise

**Expert
Systems**

Knowledge
Engineering

Types of Expert Systems
    Expert Consultants
    Job Performance Aids
    Decision Support Systems
    Articulate Expert Systems

Components of Expert Systems
    Knowledge Base
    Control Structures
    Workspace
    Interface Systems
    Explanation Subsystem

Directions

4 EXPERT SYSTEMS

Expert systems provide consultation and decision support on tasks requiring domain expertise. Expert systems are computer programs which use knowledge and information to attain and exhibit high performance levels in well-defined problem solving areas. This chapter describes how the components of expert systems work and explains the importance of this modular approach to development. The potential roles of expert systems as expert consultants, job performance aids, decision support systems, and articulate experts are explored. In addition, the value and problems of computer-based consultant systems in education and training are considered.

CONSULTING IN THE FUTURE

In the future computers may serve as consultants and guide decision making. Military research might serve as an indicator of the potential future impact of expert systems since the military has committed large amounts of money and effort to AI research and development. The Defense Advanced Research Project Agency (DARPA) has recently invested $600 million in large scale AI research projects to investigate applications. Commander Ronald Ohlander of DARPA describes his views of the Battle Management System, an AI application of the Strategic Computing Program:

> Imagine that you're in charge of achieving a *military* objective, and you have assets available at your disposal—but they're a limited resource. You have a *threat* that you have some information on, but you are also trying to gather more information. . . How do you allocate your limited resources in such a way that you can satisfy near-term objectives as well as long-term objectives and take advantages of weaknesses or strengths of what you think is going on in the external world?

133

Generally, you're trying to assign scarce resources to meet a particular objective. You never have enough of what you want. Human intuition—human judgment in decision making—certainly far surpasses the ability of any computer to make decisions in that arena now. The important thing the computer can do is to keep track of detail—how many assets you've got, how many objectives you are trying to attack—breakdowns of things that humans can't do very well at all.

My view of a *battle* management system in the future is a true symbiotic relationship between man and machine, where the machine understands very well what the human is trying to do and what his shortcomings are, and at the same time recognizes its own.

Even if the machine can understand a good part about solving the problem, to be truly useful to the human being, it has to understand part of the problem-solving task—what comes next? What does he want to see? What is the best information I could give him? So, it is not just a case of the machine going off and digesting so much input, chunking it over for a number of milliseconds or second, and spitting out an answer. It is a true interchange of information.

These problems are exceedingly difficult. Humans don't solve them that well. It requires a true interchange of information, where the human prompts for more information, and the machine anticipates what he wants and presents things in the most digestible format. (In Mishkoff, 1985, p. 237-238)

The success or failure of military products will influence the acceptance of expert systems in education and training. If successful, then educators and trainers can adapt these expert systems to provide decision making support. Alexander Romiszowski (1987), an instructional technologist, indicates that:

Expert systems have caught the attention of educators, especially the 'high-tech' fringe. Perhaps, for this reason, also, reactionary voices have been raised, questioning the educational utility, economic viability, or indeed relevance to education of expert systems. (p. 22)

Only the future will show whether the expert systems development process will provide relevant, viable, and useful products for education and training.

CONSULTING

Knowledge and information are often shared between individuals in our society. When an individual is recognized as having expertise and when that expertise is valued, that individual may become a formal or informal consultant to other individuals. Human experts are frequently in great demand and short supply. Scarcity of expertise occurs in many fields. Access to knowledge, judgment, and experience in problem solving endeavors is an invaluable asset. An understanding of the consultation process involves both a better understanding of what humans know (expertise) and how humans talk (communication). Specialized training in consultation can improve the effectiveness of this communication.

A useful distinction in viewing consulting can be made between direct and indirect services. Consultants provide an indirect service, whereas their clients provide direct services. Because of their direct service responsibilities, it is important that the consultee or client maintain a major responsibility for the solution of the problem. In the consulting approach to problem solving, the client or consultee must make the critical decisions in problem solving, and the consultant must provide assistance and support. As indicated by Reynolds and Birch (1988):

> ... the consultant does not adopt the problem but works instead to enhance the client's capacity to solve it. In so doing, the consultant may teach, do research, slow the pace, examine the organization, or do many other things to help—but always systematically. (p. 120)

Effective consulting involves managing complex relationships and realizing a mutually beneficial, collaborative effort between the consultant and the consultee.

The use of consulting in most professions and occupations is generally voluntary. However, some employers might mandate or highly recommend ineffective employees' use of the services of a consultant to try to improve their decision making. Consulting is historically viewed as the role of the most experienced, senior, or recognized expert members of a profession. Recent approaches to consultation appear to be moving toward the concept of collaboration and collegiality. This broader approach to consultation emphasizes sharing and mutual helpfulness. In addition, it emphasizes the strengths of different members or professionals in an organization. For example, in education a newer teacher with expertise in a domain such as educational computing might serve as a consultant to experienced teachers with other areas of expertise.

Human consultants are a valuable expertise and communication resource when problems arise that an individual has not previously encountered. Effective human consultants are useful and usable, can explain their advice, respond to questions, learn new knowledge, and revise their knowledge when they make errors (Waterman, 1986). Human consultants are able to apply both domain knowledge and common sense knowledge to specific problems. In addition, human experts are able to occasionally bring creativity and innovation to problem solving tasks. One important feature of human expertise is the ability to know when a problem is outside its domain.

Human resources have limits as sources of consultation. Unfortunately, human consultants with expertise in a domain are invaluable resources whose time quickly becomes limited. In addition, cost effectiveness is a critical variable in evaluating consultation. If the individual seeking assistance cannot afford the cost of consultation, then the individual will unfortunately make decisions without adequate help.

Written communication is used as a source for consultation when human experts are scarce and individual consultation is economically not feasible. Books are used by human experts to store their knowledge and expertise. Written communication is easily disseminated and stored. This expertise is a valuable resource which has traditionally been available either free or at a minimal cost through a system of libraries. The knowledge of experts is passively stored in books and written documents. As indicated by Hayes-Roth (1983):

> Although today books store the largest volume of knowledge, they merely retain symbols in a passive form. Before the knowledge stored in books can be applied, a human must retrieve it, interpret it, and decide how to exploit it for problem solving. (p. 287)

As the amount of written information is presently increasing exponentially, a need exists for other more active approaches to the transfer of expertise. Written communication does not meet all of the requirements of an effective consultant. For example, books are unable to learn new knowledge and are difficult to revise if their knowledge fails to provide effective advice. Written communication is not interactive, and is not able to respond to questions or explain advice in a flexible manner that meets the needs of individuals seeking the expertise it contains.

Computers have been proposed as interactive consultants that will provide a better linkage between human and written consulting. The interactive capabilities of the computer can provide the flexibility required for effective consultation. As with human consulting, these characteristics are equally important to those who need access to expertise and those who embody it. If effective as consultants, these computer-based consultant systems will assist with the transfer of expertise from humans to the computer to other humans. Computer-based consultants are most commonly labelled "expert systems." Expert systems may be described as "consultants that formulate opinions and give advice to users" (Barr & Feigenbaum, 1982).

Consulting is a type of problem solving behavior which involves various roles. The types of consulting which expert systems attempt to provide (which correspond to similar roles and responsibilities assume by human consultants) are listed in Table 4.1. Interpretation involves explaining observed information. Examples of interpretation in education and training are interpreting learning styles, job analysis, analyzing classroom behavior, and all types of needs and situation analyses. Prediction requires inferring the likely consequences from a given situation. Examples of prediction are achievement estimation, forecasting success rates, and resource estimation. Diagnosis involves predicting malfunctions and identifying specific problems from observed behavioral irregularities. Diagnosis attempts to relate the observed problem with the underlying causes and is an extremely common process in education and training. It is necessary to identify specific procedural errors made by students on all tasks. Design problems require construction or development of solution or mediation strategies within the constraints of a defined problem situation. Design is frequently driven by goals and objectives in education and training. Instructional design is a major area of education and training research. Planning involves designing actions for the student (Hayes-Roth, Waterman, & Lenat, 1983). Each of these consulting processes should be within the capabilities of expert systems in the future. A transfer of expertise question which must be considered is: What should an expert system know to effectively give advice? To answer this question, it is necessary to examine the various types of consulting roles and responsibilities attempted by expert systems.

TABLE 4.1

Types of Consulting Provided by Expert System

(Adapted from Hayes-Roth, Waterman, & Lenat, 1983)

Categories	Problem Areas
Interpretation	Explaining from observation information
Prediction	Inferring consequences from a situation
Diagnosis	Predicting malfunctions and identifying problems
Design	Development and construction of solutions
Planning	Designing actions

EXPERT SYSTEMS

Expert systems are computer-based consulting programs that are capable of offering advice and decision support related to specific problem solving in a well-defined knowledge domain. The development of expert systems requires that knowledge engineers work with domain experts to capture "extensive, high-quality, specific knowledge" about a specific problem solving area (Waterman, 1987). Domain knowledge or expertise relevant to the task or problem to be solved must be clarified and codified into a computer program through the processes of expert systems development. The combination of AI research and knowledge engineering has resulted in these products called "expert systems." These products can be used as stand alone computer-based systems or as components to enhance a variety of products.

Expert systems are useful tools which demonstrate the feasibility of AI applications in many domains. According to Harmon, Maus, and Morrissey (1987):

> Expert systems, with their ability to capture and distribute critical analytical and decision-making knowledge, are just the first step. They are, however, a very important step since they mark a transition between conventional approaches and the next generation of software oriented toward representing knowledge, communicating in natural languages, and reasoning by logical rather than mathematical means. (p. 10)

The modularity and flexibility of expert systems contributes to their potential utility. According to Allen and Carter (1988):

> Expert systems are most applicable when the problem domain is unstable or does not allow the entire set of methods to be specified in advance. These systems are effective problem solvers because they separate domains of knowledge from solution strategies. (p. 12)

However, the possibility of replacing human consultants with computer-based consultants requires careful evaluation.

The requirements for an effective consultant place high demands on AI research and development. If these special purpose computer programs are to act as intelligent assistants or consultants in their area of expertise, then they must demonstrate the capabilities of human expert consultants. Expert systems must meet the same criteria required of human consultants, if they are to be judged effective. The accuracy and reliability of advice is an essential requirement for effective consultation. If a human adviser frequently failed to provide either reliable or accurate advice, then, obviously, people would not seek that consultation. However, the evaluation procedures and criteria for determining whether advice is correct in advance of implementing it are difficult to identify in domains such as education where expertise is highly judgmental.

To be effective, a human or machine consultant must be articulate. Experts can explain why and how they reached a decision. They are able to teach the consultee how to solve the problem, rather than adopting the problem as their own. Occasionally, human experts are able to solve problems effectively, but cannot articulate their strategies to the extent required to perform effectively as consultants. Sometimes, an examination of the consultant's reasoning process will assist in determining the appropriateness of the advice. Good consultants are capable of explaining their logic and the sequence of their reasoning. One area of AI research, explanatory and reasoning processes required for clear communication, is likely to make significant contributions to the transfer of expertise. According to Barr and Feigenbaum (1982):

> . . . a major design issue for some of these systems, for the consultants in particular, is whether the system needs to explain its reasoning to a user. This capability is implemented primarily to convince the users that the system's reasoning is appropriate and that its conclusions about a case are reasonable. (p. 82)

Human consultants frequently forget or cannot explain their reasoning process at the level of detail needed by the novice. This explanatory process has been integrated into the capabilities of several expert systems development tools. The choice of wording in the questions and responses of the consultants play a role in their evaluation. A good consultant should be able to explain the basis for a decision and "customize" that explanation to the level of expertise of the individual seeking help. Many individuals seeking help expect the consultant to provide appropriate education at the time of decision making.

Many individuals feel that the term "expert system" is an inappropriate name for computer-based consultants. For example, Roger Schank (1984), an AI scientist, indicates:

> Expert systems are horribly misnamed, since there is very little about them that is *expert*. They are an application of current AI work on finding out what kind of knowledge people have and how to represent that knowledge. (p. 34)

The terms "knowledge system" or "knowledge-based system" are frequently used by some AI writers and by some educators and trainers. *Knowledge systems* may be defined to include a wide range of expert systems which would include both "expert consultants" that capture the heuristic expertise of experts and "job performance aids" that merely capture useful knowledge and procedures of competent performers. The term "expert systems" has been used throughout this book, not because it is necessarily a better term than knowledge systems, but because it is presently used more frequently in education and training literature. Although the connotations of the terms are different, both denote potentially exciting areas of application for education and training. Box 4.1 presents a brief history of expert systems. Box 4.2 describes recent and continuing efforts by Alan Hofmeister, Joseph Ferrara, and associates at Utah State University to develop and evaluate useful expert systems in special education.

Box 4.1

A Brief History of Expert Systems

During the 1960's AI scientists tried to find general methods of reasoning for solving broad classes of difficult problems. However, limited success with this approach began to focus researchers on domain expertise. Two early research programs which matched the performance of human experts were DENDRAL, a program that identified the chemical molecular structure of materials, and MACSYMA, a program that simplified complex mathematical expressions.

In the 1970s, AI research and development efforts confirmed the critical importance of domain knowledge and expertise on problem solving. Researchers at Stanford and other AI laboratories began to emphasize high quality and specific knowledge in well-defined problem areas. This emphasis led to successful and useful programs in applied areas such as chemistry, medicine, and geology. Since these programs attempted to capture the knowledge of experts in limited problem areas, they were called "expert systems." Edward Feigenbaum coined the term "knowledge engineering" to describe the process for capturing expertise and codifying knowledge into the knowledge-based expert system. Feigenbaum is the leader of the Stanford Heuristic Laboratory and became the founder of two commerical expert systems development companies—IntelliCorp and Teknowledge.

The first expert systems were developed by interviewing experts in specific domains such as medicine. MYCIN was an expert system developed at Stanford to consult as a specialist in diagnosing and treating specific infections. The ten years of MYCIN research have demonstrated the feasibility of capturing high level expertise (Buchanan & Shortliffe, 1984).

PROSPECTOR is an expert system developed in the late 1970's at the Stanford Research Institute to provide consultation to geologists in their exploration of sites for ore-grade deposits of precious metals. PROSPECTOR is historically interesting because during one of the early tests, PROSPEC-TOR analyzed data and identified that a previously unexplored site contained ore-grade porphyry molybdenum deposits (which had been identified as sterile by human experts). This test has led to an exploration of further commercial applications of AI and expert systems in that knowledge domain.

Several other knowledge engineering projects had accomplished significant results by the late 1970s. HEARSAY-II had combined cooperative expert systems through a "blackboard" or workspace to recognize connected speech with a 1000-word vocabulary. R1 was programmed to configure orders for Digital Equipment computers using 1000 if-then rules to demonstrate expert level performance. INTERNIST was developed as an internal medicine expert system which contained 100,000 judgments about the relationships of symptoms to diseases.

Forty AI scientists met in 1980 to collaborate on the book *Building Expert Systems*. This collaborative effort is frequently described as an important event in the history of knowledge engineering. This book is a technical, but useful source for expert systems developers. A controversial book by Feigenbaum and McCorduck, *The Fifth Generation*, describes what these authors perceive as the importance of expert systems for the economic survival of the United States.

Expert systems research and development had been confined to a few universities and research laboratories until as recently as 1980. However, development has emerged from these laboratories rapidly and has entered the commercial market with a great amount of publicity and interest. For example, Harmon, Maus, and Morrissey (1988) report that 80% of the largest companies in the United States are exploring expert systems techniques. Recent conferences on expert systems development have drawn large numbers of participants from a broad range of fields.

Box 4. 2

Expert Systems in Special Education

A series of expert systems projects has been undertaken by faculty and students at Utah State University—Technology Division of the Developmental Center for Handicapped Persons under the direction of Alan Hofmeister and Joseph Ferrara. The purpose of these expert systems are to serve as computer-based consultants in the field of special education.

Classification of handicapped students was the focus of several projects. The first project involved the development of CLASS.LD, an expert system capable of effectively classifying learning disabled students according to federal and state rules and regulations and best practices. A revised version, CLASS.LD2, uses over 200 "if-then" rules to make classifications at the level of the best experts (Hofmeister & Lubke, 1986). Follow-up classification programs have been developed for seriously emotionally disturbed or behavior disordered students (CLASS.BD/SED), physically handicapped students (CLASS.PH), communication disordered students (CLASS.SH) and mentally retarded students (CLASS.MD). Each of these expert systems has been adapted for use in several different states.

Several expert systems have been converted to computer-based simulations for use in training individuals in the classification of handicapped students. Ferrara, Prater, and Baer (1987) describe a computer-based simulation which uses an articulate expert system to teach the "multifaceted" and "dynamic" concept of "learning disabled student" to practicing teachers and administrators. Their results indicate that trainees which used the structured lesson called "L.D.Trainer" and trainees who ran special education files through the expert system "CLASS.LD" learned the complex concept of "learning disabled student." Work continues on the development of teacher training expert systems and computer-based simulation programs that combine the knowledge bases of the expert systems with a computer-based training program to automatically create a computer-based simulation.

Expert systems have been developed and evaluated by several doctoral students at Utah State Univeristy. A dissertation project by James Parry (1986) involved development and evaluation of an expert system which provides school personnel and parents with a second opinion regarding compliance and consistency of actions in the implementation of special education rules and regulations. The expert system called "Mandate Consultant" was validated and improved through systematic formative and summative evaluation procedures. This expert system program performed at levels of the "better" human experts during a "blinded" evaluation (Parry & Hofmeister, 1986). As previously indicated, Mary Ann Prater (1986) trained educators to accurately classify learning disabled students using an expert system and a computer-based simulation. Margaret Lubke (1987) developed and validated an expert system in remedial mathematics which was effectively implemented in teacher inservice. Elizabeth Martindale (1987) used an expert system to train secondary special education teachers how to plan an effective language arts lesson related to writing a letter.

On site training of student teachers is the focus of current research at Utah State University. A recently funded project from the Office of Special Education will explore the possibilities of sending expert systems in the areas of behavior management and effective teaching into the field with student teachers in special education. These expert systems will be adapted for each site to be compatible with the heuristics and rules taught by the college instructors. Initially, these expert systems will be used at sites near Utah State University, but during proceeding years of the project, they will be tested at rural sites in Idaho (Lewis Clark State College) and South Dakota (University of Sourth Dakota).

TYPES OF EXPERT SYSTEMS

Expert systems may be classified into four types based upon their purposes:
1. Expert consultants,
2. Job performance aids,
3. Decision support systems, and
4. Articulate expert systems.

Although these classifications have been arbitrarily developed to illustrate the range of expert systems, many overlaps exist among the types in real world settings. For example, expert systems may function either as an expert consultant or a job performance aid to guide a novice step-by-step or as a decision support system for an individual seeking a second opinion. Any type of expert system might function as an articulate expert system when explaining its knowledge and reasoning to a novice user or trainee.

Expert Consultants

The idea of a computer which can capture the expertise of a specialist is exciting. A major trend in our technological society has been toward specialization as is illustrated by the number of specialties in the professions of medicine and law. Specialty experts are in short supply in many areas (Harmon & King, 1985). As problems become complex, people like to turn to consultants or specialists with specialized knowledge for assistance and guidance.

Expert consultants are "intelligent" computer systems developed to achieve and perform at high levels of expertise. These expert consultants require a major development effort in attempting to capture the expertise of individuals in complex domains. Expert consultants must contain both specific knowledge of the domain and the expertise to determine when the problem is outside the expert system's area of knowledge and expertise. These "true" expert systems can serve as expert consultants when their expertise has been validated through research and development efforts. Many person years of effort are currently required to develop an expert consultant system.

Expert consultants are difficult to develop and with available technologies frequently do not perform as well as human experts except in areas where calculations and memory are critical factors. Expert consultants cannot reason broadly from general theories and deep knowledge, rather they use specific heuristics and surface knowledge. More importantly, expert consultants lack common sense. Programming common sense has proved to be a major problem for AI research. Computer-based expert consultants do not learn from experience or past mistakes. Machine learning is an area of AI research which will lead to improvements in expert systems. Present expert consultants deteriorate quickly when working outside their narrow areas of expertise (Harmon & King, 1983). As cognitive science and AI research improve the understanding of expertise, the performance of expert consultant systems will also improve. With this improvement in performance, expert consultants have the potential to significantly change education and training through using computer-based instruction concurrently with consultation.

An example of an expert consultant system which seems feasible and practical for training can be derived from a problem encountered as fuel, ignition, and regulating systems of automobiles changed from mechanical to electronic bases. The problem was that on the job mechanics and service managers had neither the expertise nor the knowledge needed to repair and troubleshoot the increasingly complex electronic systems. In some instances, the basic electronic knowledge and skills necessary to comprehend the new service manuals were lacking. If each of the electronic systems had been treated as a well-defined problem and area of expertise, the negative effects of missing prerequisite skills of service personnel would have been minimized. In addition, the levels of difficulty, frustration, consumer dissatisfaction, and the massive infusion of resources into remedial and "catch-up" training would have been reduced.

Job Performance Aids

Harmon & King (1985) make the useful distinction between small knowledge systems which serve as job performance aids and large expert systems which serve as expert consultants. *Job performance aids* or job aids are devices that individuals depend upon to perform a specific task (Harmon, Maus & Morrissey, 1988). These job aids allow students and trainees to work more accurately and more quickly, without memorizing information. Job performance aids can assist with training by providing the individual with guidance or consulting during mastery of a specific task. Instructional designers frequently select job aids to reduce training time. Romiszowski (1987) notes that:

> ....smaller systems, incorporating knowledge bases of some 20, 50, or 100 rules, are no more than glorified algorithms that can be (and indeed were) developed by non-computer techniques, such as decision-tables. (p. 22).

Examples of job performance aids are checklists, procedures manuals, and charts.

Computerized job performance aids take advantage of the interactive capabilities of the computer. Job performance aids can be rapidly developed by trainers using expert systems development tools and knowledge engineering procedures. These small knowledge systems capture the knowledge of skilled workers as they solve a semi-structured task. Small expert systems development tools are ideal for developing products such as job performance aids and will allow trainers to replace memorization requirements with "intelligent" job performance aids (Harmon & King, 1985). In addition, the development of these job performance aids will clarify the facts, rules, heuristics, and procedures required to perform the specific tasks. Small knowledge systems will have a major impact on training as computers serve the role of "intelligent" job performance aids.

Small expert systems which perform as job performance aids are sometimes referred to as knowledge systems. These knowledge systems do not perform at a high level of expertise and cannot serve as expert consultants. However, for the trainer who is required to efficiently upgrade the skill levels in a production work force with every technological advance in the production environment, small expert systems can have the precise characteristics necessary to meet the demands of that ongoing training problem.

Decision Support Systems

Decision making and decision support are currently productive areas of human and machine research. Different types of decisions require different types of support and tools. Some decisions primarily require access to information or linkage of information. Some decisions require tools for mathematical or logical analysis. Some decisions must be supported by effective graphing or visual-spatial examination. Others require a comparison of choices either by pairs or in a complex matrix.

Decision support systems (DSS) entail the use of computers as tools for aiding complex decision making. DSS are human-machine cognitive systems which represent an approach to decision making that capitalizes on the strengths of both the human and the computer while attempting to minimize the weaknesses of each. DSS augment the problem solving abilities of the decision maker. There is no consensus as to the exact meaning nor optimal components of a DSS. DSS may include expert systems components, database management programs, modeling systems, or decision analysis tools. Expert systems may be used as DSS to give second opinions or guide a decision making process rather than serving as expert consultants. A database management program with an expert system component can provide the needed information to make informed decisions and thereby be identified as a DSS.

An effective DSS provides both appropriate information and computer tools to guide educators and trainers in their decision making. As pointed out by Hayes, Pilato, and Malouf (1987):

> The human user will always bear the ultimate responsibility for intelligent decision-making, for using the specific feature of the expert system efficiently, and for cautious use of expert systems in field applications. (p. 39)

Any expert system can be used to obtain a second opinion rather than replacing humans in decision making. This system should allow the professional to construct a representation of the problem which can be manipulated to explore potential solutions. DSS support rather than replace the judgments of educators and trainers. They improve the effectiveness of decision making by allowing immediate access to the needed information while eliminating unwanted, potentially confusing and distracting information. Decision analysis tools or decision modeling tools then allow the decision maker to compare and contrast choices prior to making or implementing a decision. By providing better information and tools for analyzing choices, decision making will be significantly improved.

One goal of DSS is to provide assistance during the analysis of a decision. Decision or choice is the process by which alternatives for behavior are selected and carried out. A series of decisions is called a strategy. Consequences will result from each strategy. The task of rational decision making is to select one of the strategies which results in the preferred consequences of action (Simon, 1969). Rational decision making is a process involving the following steps:

1. Listing alternative strategies,
2. Predicting the consequences that follow the implementation of each strategy,
3. Evaluating these consequences, and
4. Choosing among alternatives (Winograd & Flores, 1986).

Decision support emphasizes an analytical and empirical approach which seems to deemphasize and avoid negative aspects of social, emotional, intuitive, and personalized approaches. Most valuable uses of decision support systems focus on alternatives, valuations, and choices. Formal models for DSS are created with sets of rules that describe the behavior of the system. Objective ways are established to assign valuations to the potential results of action, and alternatives can be compared through calculations based on the model, rules and valuations. Optimal alternatives can be selected or chosen even though all alternatives and all consequences can never be generated. Practical decision making can thereby more closely approximate the ideal. An individual cannot predict all consequences because these consequences are in the future. Values can only be estimated. In real-world situations, all possible alternatives cannot be considered (Simon, 1976) and that end is not likely to be realized by the use of DSS.

Semi-structured tasks are ideally suited to computerized decision analysis tools. Structured tasks allow for algorithmic procedures which can be implemented in a traditional computer program. For completely unstructured tasks, rules cannot be formulated, and computers may not be useful. The tasks in between may be called semi-structured, and have only a limited degree of predictability (Winograd & Flores, 1986). Given the current status of expert systems development, knowledge domains, and in-field practices of educators and trainers, the emergence of DSS may well be the most promising avenue of AI applications in the semi-structured task domain of designing effective instruction.

Articulate Expert Systems

Articulate expert systems are computer-based consultants that can explain their reasoning processes. The ability to explain its reasoning to a novice user may be a role of consultation where expert systems can be systematically more effective than human consultants. This is of tremendous importance in education and training as the acquisition of increasing levels of expertise, in an efficient and effective manner, is a career long need of educators and trainers. Having intermittent and irregular access to a human consultant with incredibly well developed expertise who cannot or will not reveal the underlying reasoning processes is among the more frustrating experiences encountered by novice instructors and instructional designers.

Articulate expert systems may be classified as either a type of expert system or a type of intelligent computer-assisted instruction (ICAI) system (Kearsley, 1987). Articulate expert systems are computer consulting systems which have the capabilities of explaining their reasoning and explicitly showing their knowledge base. The programs have been called glass-box experts because their reasoning is inspectable by students (Goldstein & Papert, 1977). Articulate expert systems provide the capabilities of explaining why the consultant program has asked a question, showing the rules used in the search for solutions, and assigning confidence factors to alternative solutions.

Presently, most articulate expert systems are rule-based expert systems which can explain their reasoning. Using articulate expert systems, individuals can be guided through the decision making process while tracing the reasoning of the computer consultant. Most expert systems being developed have this capability—so most current expert systems are articulate expert systems. These articulate expert systems are useful as a stand alone ICAI, but have more potential as the expertise module of an ICAI program. As previously noted, articulate expert systems may be developed and evaluated prior to use as the expertise module in an ICAI program. If this content is established as a separate module, then articulate expert systems provide a clear source of information such as rules, objects, attributes, heuristics, examples, or values which will guide instructional design analysis. These expert systems, then, may serve as the declarative, procedural, and heuristic knowledge in an ICAI program.

Although the GUIDON program described in Chapter One serves as the classic example of converting an expert system to an ICAI system, educators and trainers are beginning to use microcomputer-based expert system development tools to create articulate expert systems for training purposes. For example, McFarland, Ragan, McFarland, and Kottkey (1987) developed an articulate expert system for training student nurses to interpret blood gas testing results. By using a range of cases involving simple to complex test results, they were able to improve the student nurses' abilities to interpret laboratory reports and make appropriate nursing care decisions.

COMPONENTS OF EXPERT SYSTEMS

One important technique of planning and programming in AI is modularity. Expert systems are developed through a modular approach. Modularity is the division of major components into subcomponents and then into elements. Modularity allows for easier development and evaluation of a system. Harmon, Maus, and Morrissey (1988) indicate the importance of modularity in expert systems:

> The separation of knowledge from inference and control is probably the most important concept to come out of AI research. (p. 8)

For example, an expert system can be modified by merely changing elements such as rules in the knowledge base. The modularity of the domain knowledge in the knowledge base makes the revision of prototypes simpler during the expert systems development process. Since many expert systems development tools provide all other components, only changes in the rules or facts are required to improve the performance of the prototype expert system. Expert systems differ from conventional computer programming approaches in that the domain knowledge is separated from the control and reasoning system.

The modular approach allows for the description of an ideal expert system with the following main components:

1. Knowledge base,
2. Control structures,
3. Workspace,
4. Interface systems, and
5. Explanation subsystem.

The knowledge base may use one or more of the types of knowledge representation systems described in Chapter Two. The control structures may be subdivided into the scheduler, the interpreter, and the consistency enforcer. The workspace may store different types of intermediate decisions. The interface systems may be subdivided into the user interface, the explanation subsystem, and other interfaces with outside sources of information. These components and their subcomponents as shown in Figure 4.1 will be described to clarify the functioning of an expert system during a consultation. Current expert systems do not have all of these components and subcomponents. Future descriptions of ideal expert systems may add other components and subcomponents to their model (Kinnucan, 1984).

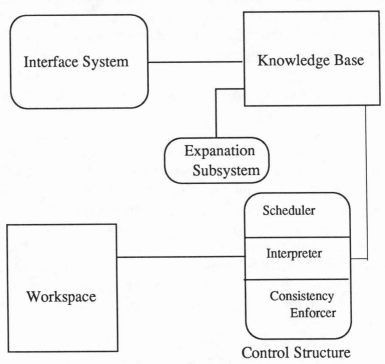

FIGURE 4. 1
Components of an Ideal Expert System
(Adapted from Hayes-Roth, Waterman, & Lenat, 1983)

Knowledge Base

The *knowledge base* is the "repository" of domain knowledge in the expert system (Hayes-Roth, Waterman, and Lenat, 1983). This component of an expert system consists of the facts (or data) and rules or other knowledge representations containing the heuristics about the domain or problem solving task (Waterman, 1986). The knowledge base may be represented by any of the knowledge representation techniques described in Chapter Two. Presently, the most common type of expert system is a rule-based expert system or production system. In a rule-based expert system, the knowledge base consists of facts and heuristic rules that represent expert level decision making. With the increasing availability of sophisticated expert systems development tools, hybrid systems are being used to codify domain knowledge. This collection of facts, rules, and heuristics is provided to the computer program by the domain expert and encoded by the knowledge engineer.

The use of appropriate domain knowledge is of critical importance to expert systems if they are to consult effectively. The most useful component of an expert system is the knowledge base. According to Waterman (1986):

> The heart of an expert system is the powerful corpus of knowledge that accumulated during system building. The knowledge is explicit and organized to simplify decision making. . . It has the value that any large body of knowledge has and can be widely disseminated via books and lectures. (p. 6-7)

This knowledge base can also provide an institutional memory of current policies, opinions, consensus, and operating procedures. Waterman (1986) projects that knowledge bases will become a valuable resource in the future:

> One of the most important by-products of this expert systems development will be the codification of knowledge. As developers construct large, sophisticated knowledge bases, a market will develop for the knowledge itself, independent of the associated computer systems. Tutoring facilities will be developed to help disseminate this information to students trying to learn about the application domain and "knowledge decompilers" will be designed to translate the knowledge bases into coherent books or written reports. (p. 220)

The growing sophistication of expert systems development tools described in the previous chapter has enabled incorporation of all components except the knowledge base into these tools. The knowledge engineer needs to provide only the knowledge base to develop an expert system if an appropriate tool can be selected for the task of expert systems development.

Box 4.3

Knowledge Base and Database

Knowledge bases and databases are two concepts which are difficult to differentiate because of overlapping label use and descriptive similarities. Both knowledge bases and databases are used to store information. For example, knowledge engineers store knowledge which is highly structured, organized, and interconnected through knowledge representation systems in an expert system. Traditionally, computers have stored information in a structured database for retreival when access to specific information is required. To further confuse the concepts, some AI and computer scientists use the terms interchangeably. However, most knowledge engineers differentiate the terms. According to Rauch-Hindin (1988):

> Both knowledge bases and traditional databases are designed to store information. They differ significantly from each other in the types of information they can store, and the types of interrelationships between data they can handle. (p. 45-46)

The conventional database is used to store facts in a predetermined structure. Databases require rigid structures and explicitly ordered storage of facts in specified fields. Once databases are developed and stored through the use of database management procedures and database management programs such as Dbase IV, changing the format or relationships of fields is extremely difficult and may result in loss of information. Queries to a database return specific reports. Databases are not able to handle complex descriptions involving causal relationships or uncertain knowledge about stored facts.

In contrast, knowledge bases developed with expert systems development tools represent knowledge and information in a flexible and modular structure which allows for alteration of facts and interrelationships. Like the database, the knowledge base stores facts, but in addition is capable of storing cause-effect relationships, rules, and imprecise knowledge (Rauch–Hindin, 1988). For example, the facts and rules may be modified "on the fly" as the computer system attempts to solve the problem with rules having the capabilities of temporarily or permanently modifying facts or other rules in the knowledge base (Harris & Davis, 1986).

The ability to differentiate applications for expert systems development and database management may become more useful in the future as new types of tools emerge. In addition, several of the new expert systems development tools allow for linkage of databases and expert systems. The database becomes the area in which the computer system stores facts and information and the expert system provides the flexibility to use this information in problem solving. The knowledge base in the expert system then stores the rules and other knowledge representation techniques for the interconnections required for domain problem solving. When the expert system needs information, it seeks this information in the separate data base. This separation of the knowledge base and database allows for development of the database using a database management system and development of the knowledge base using an expert systems development tool. These modular systems which combine approaches to knowledge and information are frequently labelled "decision support systems."

Control Structures

The control structures may be developed by the knowledge engineer in an AI language or found in the expert systems development tools. The control structures are responsible for processing the domain knowledge in the knowledge base to seek solutions (Waterman, 1986). Often these control structures are further subdivided into levels of control. For example, they may be subdivided into the scheduler, the interpreter, and the consistency enforcer levels (Hayes-Roth, Waterman, & Lenat, 1983).

Scheduler. The scheduler is the planner which is sometimes called the control mechanism. The scheduler attempts to organize the overall approach to solving the problem at a strategic level. The scheduler is the section of a computer program that "drives" the system. The scheduler uses control mechanisms to determine the order of inference.

Interpreter. The interpreter is frequently called the inference engine in expert systems development. The interpreter attempts to solve the problem at the tactical level as it is the component of the expert system which contains the inference procedures. These inference procedures draw conclusions and make recommendations about a problem presented to the system. As described in Chapter Two, the *inference engine* makes inferences from information provided by the user or provided in the knowledge base. The interpreter is that part of the expert system which uses machine reasoning strategies. For example, many rule-based expert systems such as MYCIN use the machine reasoning strategies of backward chaining as described in the production system example of Chapter Two.

Consistency Enforcer. The consistency enforcer implements "truth-maintenance procedures" using numerical adjustments in belief. Confidence factors for expert systems' judgements are assigned by the consistency enforcer. In some instances, when the confidence assigned falls below a desired level, the expert systems will reject a rule or segment of knowledge. In other instances, as the confidence level increases, a rule or segment of knowledge significantly influences the interpreter or the scheduler. Otherwise, the confidence levels will be shown with all possible solutions to the problem that the system generates.

Workspace

The workspace (sometimes called the blackboard) is used by the expert system to record intermediate results, hypotheses, and decisions. The control structures access these intermediate results as the expert system works toward a solution or solutions to the problems. The scheduler of the control structures maintains an agenda for actions in the workspace. The interpreter uses the workspace to record intermediate findings and solutions. The consistency enforcer records numerical results related to levels of confidence assigned to solutions in the workspace.

The workspace is sometimes compared to short-term memory in human problem solving. For example, in a production system, the workspace is a working short-term memory which identifies rules that have succeeded or failed, as well as the the cumulative certainty factor for each potential solution. Another analogy for the workspace is the "blackboard" on which intermediate results and hypotheses are temporarily recorded. These temporary results change as the control mechanism seeks to solve the problem. For example, intermediate findings and potential solutions are erased and replaced by other findings and solutions as new information is added to the knowledge base. This analogy is similar to a human problem solver recording, erasing, and changing results on a blackboard as he or she seeks to solve a problem. Some expert systems development tools allow the user to observe changing results on this "blackboard."

Interface

Expert systems development tools and the resulting expert systems products vary greatly in the degree of support and interaction provided by the interface systems. For example, some expert systems development tools provide features such as on-line help, graphic displays, natural language interactions, and explanation facilities (Harmon, Maus, & Morrissey, 1988). How the user interacts with the computer-based consulting system is largely the result of the interface system provided by the expert systems development tool. AI research and development efforts have resulted in user-friendly and graphic interfaces like those found on the Macintosh computer. Although individuals developing expert systems directly in AI languages will be able to adapt and improve the user interface, most educators and trainers will merely utilize the interface system as provided by the tool.

The interface between the computer and the user is critical for an effective expert system. Harmon and King (1985) describe the interface as:

> The link between a computer program and the outside world. A single program may have several interfaces. Knowledge systems typically have interfaces for development (the knowledge acquisition interface) and the users (the user interface). In addition, some systems have interfaces that pass information to and from other programs, data bases, display devices, or sensors. (p. 261)

Graphic Interface. The user interface may include graphic features to improve communications with the user. Recent research in expert systems and intelligent computer-assisted instruction (ICAI) has focused on improving the graphic interface. For example, the GUI-DON program of research and development described in Chapter One has recently focused efforts on a GUIDON-WATCH graphic and windows interface. GUIDON-WATCH now includes features such as pull-down menus, on-line help, use of a mouse selection device, and many types of windows. For example, GUIDON-WATCH includes a positive findings window, a differential window, a diagnostic task tree window, and a hypotheses-with-evidence window (Richer & Clancey, 1985). Another excellent example of graphic interface research is STEAMER, the interactive inspectable simulation described in Box 5.5 of Chapter Five.

Natural Language Interface. Natural language interactions would be an ideal goal for human consultation. AI research and development attempts in natural language understanding and translating between human languages resulted in a major failure to achieve established goals within timelines. However, recent research and development efforts in developing natural language "front ends" for databases have been more successful. Natural language processors that parse and interpret the questions, answers, and commands typed by the user are incorporated into many expert systems development tools. This capability is possible because of the limited vocabulary in a domain of expertise. However, the capabilities of these natural language interface systems are severely limited at present. Some expert systems development tools utilize menu and graphic features to replace or supplement natural language interactions.

Speech Recognition Interface. The speech recognition area of AI research is pursuing development of computers that can understand human speech. Speech recognition has unfortunately become a complex area of computer technology which is unlikely to achieve breakthoughs in the near future. At present, some computer systems are able to recognize restricted vocabularies from restricted sets of speakers. Only a few commercial programs are available at present and these computer programs must be trained to recognize the speech patterns and the vocabulary of the user. Some interface systems emphasize sound recognition as a critical field of AI application. *Sound recognition* involves processing and reasoning about acoustic sensory information from alarms or monitoring devices. Sound recognition involves the interpretation of audible sounds and may be defined to include voice prints and speech recognition (Carrico, Girard, & Jones, 1989).

Device Interfaces. Other interface systems are required if the expert system is to effectively communicate with external sensor devices, databases, or media devices. Several expert systems development tools provide the capabilities of this external linkage. For example, some expert systems seek information and record solutions in an external database. Other expert systems are able to control a videodisc player and show videodisc segments when accessed by a specific rule such as "If answer is yes, then begin video at frame 1111." As shown in Figure 4.1, an explanation subsystem must connect to the interface system.

Explanation Subsystem

An explanation facility is the part of the expert system that explains how solutions are being sought or arrived at, and justifies the steps used in the process of reaching them. Explanation is the information presented to the user to justify the reasoning or actions of the expert system. For example, the expert systems development tool, M.1, permits the user to ask "Why," "Show," or "Trace on." The expert system then responds by showing goals, rules, or canned responses which reveal the processes of inference.

A major design issue for the future development and expanded use of expert systems is having the capability of explaining the reasoning process used in solving problems in the domain of expertise. According to Barr and Feigenbaum (1982):

> These systems require a representational formalism capable of supporting the reasoning and explanatory abilities that would closely approximate the conceptual framework of the expert and the end user. (p. 82)

Many expert systems include sophisticated capabilities for communicating their knowledge to the user. The usefulness of expert systems with explanatory capabilities is obvious to educators and trainers. This usefulness and value increases if the expert system can function as an expert consultant, explain its reasoning process, and communicate its knowledge to a novice.

Many expert systems provide the capabilities of explaining why the consultant program has asked a question, showing the rules used in the search for solutions, and assigning confidence factors to each solution. At present, most expert systems with explanatory subsystems are rule-based and can explain their reasoning through a sharing of rules used in the decision process. By using articulate expert systems, individuals can learn aspects of decision making while being guided through the decision process or tracing the system's reasoning.

CHAPTER SUMMARY

• Consulting is a problem solving behavior that may involve interpretation, prediction, diagnosis, design, or planning. Consultants provide collaborative and indirect services to the consultee who is responsible for decision making. Consultation may be provided by humans, written communication, or computers. Computers are proposed as interactive consultants that provide a linkage between human and written problem solving and consultation.

• Expert systems are computer-based consulting programs which provide advice and decision support in well-defined knowledge domains. To be effective consultants, expert systems must be able to provide high quality domain expertise and articulate why and how they have made specific decisions. The types of expert systems are computer-based expert systems including expert consultant systems, computerized job performance aids, and decision support systems.

• Expert consultant systems are able to perform at high levels of expertise. Expert consultants require a major effort involving one or more domain experts and knowledge engineers and the best available AI tools and languages. Research on expertise and common sense is attempting to improve the functioning of expert consultant systems.

• Job performance aids are devices that assist individuals by providing information and a reminder of steps in the procedure during the performance of a specific and useful task. Small expert systems can serve as computerized job performance aids. These systems are easily developed with the help of expert systems development tools.

• Decision making by humans and computers is an area of AI application with implications for education and training. Decision support systems use computers to guide individuals in the decision making process. Decision support systems manage information and specialized knowledge to optimize effective choices by listing alternative strategies and evaluating consequences. These decision support systems include expert systems components, database management programs, modeling systems, and decision support tools.

• The components of an expert system are the knowledge base, the control structures, the workspace, and the interface system. The modular approach to the development of expert systems allows for easy design and revision often requiring changes only in the knowledge base.

• The knowledge base consists of facts, rules, and other knowledge representation techniques which contain the heuristics about the problem solving task. This explicit and accessble knowledge is a useful component in that it provides an institutional memory, current policies, and operating procedures.

• The control structures include the scheduler, interpreter, and consistency enforcer. The scheduler plans the overall approach to solving the problem at the strategic level. The interpreter is the inference engine that solves the problem, draws conclusions, and makes recommendations through a machine reasoning process such as backward chaining. The consistency enforcer implements truth maintence procedures using numerical adjustments such as confidence factors.

• The workspace is used as a "blackboard" by the expert system to record intermediate results, hypotheses, and decisions. The workspace provides a short-term memory for storing the constantly change results during the machine reasoning process.

• Interfaces are the links between the computer and the outside world. An expert system might have graphic, natural language, and speech recognition, and device interfaces. Graphic interfaces provide use of a mouse selection device, windows, pull-down menus, and point and click features. Natural language interfaces allow interactions through question and answer formats similar to communications with humans through writing or speaking. Speech recognition allows the computer to understand human speech. External sensor devices, databases, or media devices may be used as interfaces with the computer.

SCORECARD				
Will AI Research and Development Efforts Contribute to Education and Training?				
Topic	Question Dimensions			
	Feasibility	Improved Effectiveness	Capacity Enhancing	Future Utility
Consulting				
Expert Systems				
Expert Consultants				
Job Performance Aids				
Decision Support Systems				
Articulate Expert Systems				
Knowledge Base				
Control Structure				
Interface System				
Explanation Subsystem				

Comments:

DIRECTIONS

Consulting with computers in the future raises many exciting possibilities. Expert systems are proposed as an innovative computer technology from the field of AI which will significantly improve education and training. If expert systems can be provided with a large, relevant body of educational and training knowledge, they can provide decision support or consultation to teachers and trainers. At the same time, the idea of a computer as an expert consultant, job performance aid, and decision support system raises a number of interesting questions for educators and trainers. While these questions cannot be answered at present, answers will become clearer as AI research and development emerges from the laboratories. Let us consider a few.

Would educators and trainers use expert systems if they were available and performed as effectively as consultants? To answer this question we must extrapolate from present uses of humans and written materials as consultants. Many educators and trainers are reluctant to use human consultants to help solve specific problems due to a number of factors. Few specialists are recognized in education and training. Unlike the medical and law professions, most educators and trainers are responsible for a broad range of work tasks within the areas of instructional delivery, management of instruction, developing materials, and assessment of learners. In additon, educators and trainers such as classroom teachers, professors, and military trainers are frequently considered to be equal according to the responsibilities assigned in the instructional setting regardless of seniority, rank, or expertise. Further, the systems in which they operate expect them to perform as experts and often negatively evaluate them if they formally request access to consultants. Although educators and trainers seek workshops for general problem solving assistance, limited economic resources and institutional constraints have not permitted the emergence of consultants on site, or easy off-site access to them, for most educators and trainers.

Written materials are not presently able to focus solutions upon specific problems because of the complexity of variables involved in most training or education settings. Most written materials which attempt to consult must use a linear, step-by-step approach to problem solving. This linear approach is likely to systematically manifest oversimplification which is unlikely to help solve the complex problems of education and training. Furthermore, it is likely to exclude those problems from penetrating analysis. These how-to-do-it books and articles are an important source of information and consultation in many areas, but professionals such as educators and trainers frequently have not responded well to them. For example, although many parents will purchase books on discipline and motivation with a how-to-do-it emphasis, professionals realizing the complexity of discipline and motivation are more cynical about the levels of success to be attained by applying such "cookie-cutter" approaches.

If the problem solving advice and decision support of a recognized expert in education and training were available by subscription, would many individuals subscribe? For example, if the expertise of Robert M. Gagne and/or M. David Merrill were captured in a computer program containing their advice on developing an effective lesson to teach a defined concept, would educators and trainers follow their heuristics and seek further clarification when they encounter problems from that computer consultation? Would they subscribe to a service in which they could continue to receive revised expert systems from instructional designers?

Education and training novices are all too frequently negatively influenced by experienced practitioners regarding the usefulness of the knowledge they learned during pre-service training. This negativism delays the use of innovation by novices in the field. Some of this resistance may be responsible for the ten year research-discovery-to-field-adoption timeline expected for experienced practitioners. Rarely is the novice trainer or educator in an initial job placement for a week following completion of a professional preparation program (all too often it happens during practicum experiences) without receiving the advice from more experienced colleagues to " . . . forget all that theoretical and research stuff now because you're in the real world." Without strong conviction, outside support, contrary advice, or some combination of the foregoing, the novice may begin to actively repress the knowledge base gained through professional preparation and conform to the mores and norms of nay-saying colleagues. Access to expert systems as decision support systems or consultants during professional preparation programs, orientation experiences, and the initial years of service as a novice should function to overcome the negative effects of well meant, but destructive advice. In addition, the decision support capabilities of expert systems might reduce the research-discovery-to-field-adoption interval for best practices and validated research findings. Novice trainers and educators, given such access conditions, might ironically bring innovations to experienced colleagues by demonstrating their utility and practicality for their shared "real world."

The computer has demonstrated potential to be a useful consulting, decision support, and job performance aid tool for educators and trainers. Small knowledge systems have demonstrated utility in well-defined areas of decision making. In the near future, expert-consultant computers will be of even greater assistance. Knowledge engineering is emerging as a profession which is complementary to instructional design and will assist with the development of expert systems and computer consulting programs in all professions.

The future of expert systems is viewed optimistically by many books in the field of AI. A survey of professional journals, popular literature, and computer magazines indicates an increasing interest in expert systems. Expert systems have demonstrated effectiveness in areas such as medicine, law, military science, science, and agriculture. There is no conceivable technical reason, certainly not a lack of need, nor is there a lack of expertise that would prevent expert systems from becoming an important tool for educators and trainers. Is there reason for this optimism? The recent development of easy to use expert system development tools for microcomputers increases the feasibility of expert systems emerging in educational and training settings. Also, the development of megabyte storage for microcomputers increases the feasibility and affordability of sophisticated expert systems in education and training. Recent prototype systems have been developed in the following areas of interest to educators and trainers:

1. Diagnosis and classifying of exceptional learners,
2. Consultation related to due process procedures,
3. Assessment of skill strengths and weaknesses,
4. Recommendation of behavioral intervention,
5. Material evaluation and selection advice, and
6. Recommendations to increase instructional effectiveness.

Expert systems should be considered to be more than just products. The processes of expert systems development lead to clarification of knowledge and expertise. Expert systems involve a set of concepts and techniques that will enable individuals to use computers in a unique way (Harmon, Maus, & Morrissey, 1988). These unique computer applications may be developed by knowledge engineers with backgrounds in education and training and will become more widespread as expert systems development tools become easier to use and widely available. Better interface systems are being provided for users and developers as the quality of expert systems development tools improves. As described in Chapter Three, expert systems development tools are significantly improving with each revision or new product. These tools will soon provide user interfaces for microcomputer workstations with all the features being explored by the GUIDON-WATCH and STREAMER projects.

The roles of educators and trainers overlap with those of

the consultant. As consultants, educators and trainers must diagnose observed behavioral irregularities and classify these irregularities into potential causal categories. They are frequently called upon to provide assistance and guidance in areas of instructional planning and design. For example, if the expertise of the best instructional designers could be captured in a computer program, then this computer program could be consulted frequently during planning for instruction by novice instructional designers, educators, and trainers. Consulting is an important role for educators and trainers, and all of us frequently profit from consultation during planning or developing instruction. One approach to disseminating the needed level of advice is computer delivered consultation.

Many of the problems encountered in a teaching-training environment could be solved if an expert consultant was always available to assist with planning, classification, and design. Obviously, the costs and feasibility of having a human consultant with the appropriate expertise is prohibitive in most situations. If a computer consultant could develop the same or a similar level of expertise, it could be always available when problems emerged. The utility of an expert system for novice educators and trainers may be proven even if its performance level is below that of the best human consultants. Novices will perform better by using the expert system than they can without it. Given the timeline for development of expertise, an expert system which might not raise the performance level of a 10-year veteran trainer would be likely to do that for the novice. Expert systems as consultants have exciting implications for education and training.

TOPICAL REFERENCES

Consulting

Reynolds, M.C., & Birch, J.W. (1988). *Adaptive mainstreaming—A primer for teachers and principals*. New York: Longman.

Expert Systems

Feigenbaum, E.A., & McCorduck, P. (1983). *The fifth generation— Artificial intelligence and Japan's challenge to the world*. Reading, MA: Addison-Wesley Publishing.

Hayes-Roth, F., Waterman, D.A., & Lenat, D.B. (1983). *Building expert systems*. Reading, MA: Addison-Wesley Publishing.

Harmon, P., & King, D. (1985). *Expert Systems—Artificial intelligence in business*. New York: John Wiley & Sons.

Harris, L.R., & Davis, D.B. (1986). *Artificial intelligence enters the marketplace*. Toronto: Bantam Books.

Van Horn, M. (1986). *Understanding expert systems*. Toronto: Bantam Books.

Williamson, M. (1986). *Artificial intelligence for microcomputers— The guide for business decisionmakers*. New York: Brady Communication Company.

Expert Consultants

Waterman, DA. (1986). *A guide to expert systems*. Reading, MA: Addison-Wesley Publishing.

Weiss, S.M. (1984). *A practical guide to designing expert systems*. Totowa, NJ: Rowman & Allanheld.

Job Performance Aids

Harmon, P., & King, D. (1985). *Expert systems—Artificial intelligence in business*. New York: John Wiley & Sons.

Harmon, P., Maus, R., & Morrissey, W. (1988). *Expert systems tools and applications*. New York: John Wiley & Sons.

Romiszowski, A.J. (1987). Expert systems in education and training: Automated job aids or sophisticated instructional media, *Educational Technology, 27* (10), 22-30.

Decision Support Systems

Shelly,G.B., & Cashman, T.J. (1984). *Computer fundamentals for an information age*. Brea, CA: Anaheim Publishing.

Winograd, T., & Flores, F. (1987). *Understanding computers and cognition—A new foundation*. Reading, MA: Addison-Wesley Publishing.

Articulate Expert Systems

Kearsley, G. (Ed.) (1987). *Artificial intelligence and instruction—Applications and methods*. Reading, MA: Addison-Wesley Publishing.

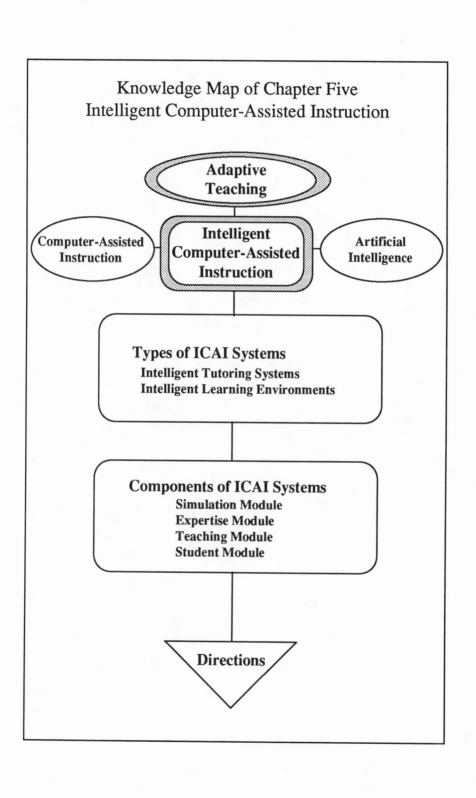

Knowledge Map of Chapter Five
Intelligent Computer-Assisted Instruction

Adaptive
Teaching

Computer-Assisted
Instruction

Intelligent
Computer-Assisted
Instruction

Artificial
Intelligence

Types of ICAI Systems
Intelligent Tutoring Systems
Intelligent Learning Environments

Components of ICAI Systems
Simulation Module
Expertise Module
Teaching Module
Student Module

Directions

5 INTELLIGENT COMPUTER-ASSISTED INSTRUCTION

Intelligent computer-assisted instruction (ICAI) systems are applications of AI which attempt to enhance education and training through research in learning environments, adaptive teaching, use of domain expertise, and diagnosis of student learning. The range of applications in ICAI is illustrated by examples from the general categories of intelligent learning environments and intelligent tutoring systems (ITS). Intelligent learning environments are microworlds, simulations, and hypermedia environments which when merged with ITS allow student exploration with "intelligent" monitoring and coaching. Classic ITS prototypes such as mixed initiative dialogues, diagnostic tutors and computer coaches demonstrate capabilities for adaptive teaching which complement previous research studies in computer-based adaptive instructional systems. Four components of ICAI are the emphases of current research and development: the simulation module, the expertise module, the teaching module, and the student module. The influences of AI and computer-assisted instruction (CAI) are examined to determine their potential impact upon ICAI.

ADAPTIVE TEACHING IN THE FUTURE

William Clancey (1987), the developer of the GUIDON program described in Chapter One, states his perception of ICAI in the future:

> The confluence of problem-solving research, inexpensive computers, and bit-map graphics is a most exciting development, and the pragmatic as well as the philosophic effects are generally yet to be realized. In this rapidly-changing field, we should expect dramatic changes in future research goals and assumptions, concerning what instructional programs are in theory capable of doing and what kinds of aids are believed to be worth considering. (p. 248)

177

According to Clancey (1987), the critical question that educators and trainers must answer is:

> What unique advantages does AI and knowledge engineering bring to teaching? (p. 246)

Will innovative AI and computer technologies dramatically improve adaptive teaching and learning environments in the future? M. David Merrill (1988), CAI researcher and instructional designer, suggests that:

> The real question is whether the computer allows us to implement instructional strategies that would be difficult or impossible to implement with live teachers. If so then we may demonstrate that the more easily implemented instructional strategy or content representation leads to an improvement in learning rather than the fact that it was implemented via a computer. (p . 7)

The use of sophisticated AI programming techniques and tools does not assure effective instruction or better learning environments. The potential of ICAI research and development is more likely to be achieved through the collaborative efforts of professionals from education, training, AI, cognitive science, and computer science. The computer, with multimedia enhancements, provides the potential for powerful learning environments and effective tutoring. As indicated by educators, Robert Tennyson and Joseph Ferrara (1987):

> . . . we can now do our job of determining where and how these AI tools can be used to enhance our instructional systems. And, more importantly, we can have the time to do the necessary basic research to sort out the variables and strategies that can be shown both theoretically and empirically to improve learning. (p. 8)

To be powerful and effective in adaptive teaching, a concurrent development process of knowledge engineering and instructional design must be extended to the planning, design, construction, and evaluation of ICAI systems.

ADAPTIVE TEACHING

Adaptive teaching, adaptive education, and adaptive instruction are vogue terms which are frequently used by educators and trainers both synonymously and in different ways to describe individualized approaches to education and training. General agreement seems to exist that adaptation is required for optimal and individualized instruction. *Adaptive teaching* may be defined as optimal instructional adaptations that effectively meet the individual needs of the students while they are actively working in controllable learning environments. This definition encompasses the concerns of Glaser (1977) for the development of competence in alternative environments matched to differing styles of learning. In addition, this definition includes the focus on teaching strategies for prescribing the optimal variables for instruction to achieve a given objective (Tennyson & Park, 1984).

In the future, the challenge of individual needs and differences will be met by a combination of training and education. Training may be delivered on a highly individualized basis through motivating drill and practice, "intelligent" tutoring, and powerful simulations. Training would center on the learner's need for "real world" expertise and would emphasize specific tasks and procedures. Education would stress human roles and needs such as interpersonal relationships, critical interpretation, and creative activities. Education may be delivered in groups or on a one-to-one basis by human teachers with adaptive teaching assistance and learning environment enhancements from computers and multimedia tools (Dede, 1983).

Education and training overlap in numerous ways and boundaries which are said to exist between these two approaches become less distinct upon close, objective examination. Romiszowski (1981) notes that:

> As most training involves some unplanned learning (educational effects) and most education involves some planned, goal-oriented teaching (i.e., training) the value of these two terms as discriminators is somewhat dubious. . .The use of the term 'instruction' may help to both distinguish and unite the two processes. (p. 4)

Examining the existence and appropriateness of varying approaches to adaptive teaching and individualized instruction serves to illustrate the fuzzy nature of these supposed boundaries between education and training.

Adaptive teaching is a major topic of research in education and training. Adaptive teaching research focuses on variables that can be manipulated by teachers or computers to control the learning environment and respond to the individual needs of each student. Tennyson and Park (1984) indicate that the goals of adaptive teaching are the implementation of diagnostic and prescriptive instructional systems designed to make learning more efficient, meaningful, and productive and to facilitate acquisition of specified objectives.

Systematic procedures for instructional adaptation have not been clearly established and validated (Corno & Snow, 1987). According to Ohlsson (1987):

> Proponents of individualized instruction, or as it is sometimes called, adaptive education, have sought to tailor instruction to such characteristics of the student as initial competence, educational goal, learning style, and, most often, learning rate, in recognition of the fact that interindividual differences in cognition implies that different learners need different instruction. Neither the history not the current state of such efforts are encouraging. (p. 203)

Because of the cognitive, logistic, and behavioral requirements of group teaching responsibilities, most educators and trainers cannot provide the needed diagnosis and correction for effective adaptive teaching. Without major restructuring, adaptive teaching remains an unfulfilled promise in education and training. Adaptations in curriculum and instruction in present educational and training settings do not meet the demands placed upon them by student variations and resource differences across settings. To achieve specific objectives and meet individual needs, two levels of adaptation must be considered.

Macroadaptation

One level of adaptive teaching is called macroadaptation. *Macroadaptation* represents the month-to-month, curriculum and program level decisions required for achievement of common and individual goals in the course or units. These long-term decisions should be responsive to both cognitive and affective measures taken prior to instruction. Examples of cognitive measures would include the constructs of intelligence, aptitude, ability, and cognitive style. Affective measures might include personality characteristics, learning styles, motivation, and anxiety.

Educators and trainers vary widely in their ability to perform macroadaptation and long-term planning. Corno and Snow (1986) indicate that:

> A wide spectrum of adaptive teaching can be observed in the behavior of many classroom teachers. (p. 612)

Not surprisingly, findings reveal that differences between "best practices" and "poor practices" are significant and have been frequently observed among teachers within the same setting. Unfortunately, most research on macroadaptation has been confounded by the complexity of variables involved in classroom teaching. For example, this confounding has led to controversy and confusion regarding the findings of aptitude-treatment interaction (ATI) research and the recent research based on learning styles inventories. In addition, this research has emphasized public school classrooms with few studies of other education and training settings.

Some educators and trainers have become disillusioned with attempts at macroadaptation. They recommend that macroadaptations be minimized and that emphasis be focused upon effective instruction. For example, Bunderson (1970) recommended that the best instructional program be maximized by evaluation methods prior to adapting it to the moment-by-moment needs of individual students. Meeting the moment-to-moment needs of the student requires an additional level of adaptation.

Microadaptation

Microadaption comprises the moment-to-moment decisions required to attend to the step-by-step processes of systematic instruction. Microadaptation requires that the instructional amount, pacing, sequence, feedback, reinforcement, and other activities be adapted to the unique needs of each learner (Tennyson, Christensen, & Park, 1984). Attention to the details of instruction required for microadaptation is a major focus of instructional technology and instructional design research. Instructional technology combines the study of instructional media, individualized instruction, and systematic development of instruction (Gagne, 1987). Most research on the systematic development of instruction or instructional design examines the decisions required for microadaptations. From this research, positive findings about how to adapt in moment-by-monent instruction are emerging (Dede & Swigger, 1988).

Unfortunately, educators and trainers in "live" group settings are unable to attend to the moment-by-moment decisions of microadaptation which would enable "true" individualized instruction. For example, most current teaching is delivered by "standup lecture supplemented by print materials" (Merrill, 1988). This combination of lecture and print delivery limits the options for individualized adaptation.

Even on a one-to-one basis, a condition considered optimal for teaching, the feasibility of systematically making effective microadaptations is limited to the extent that an instructor's level of expertise in instructional design, presentation, and management matches the additive demands of the learner's characteristics and the environment. Teacher behaviors during observation within each kind of classroom activity reveal variance in presenting lesson information, soliciting student responses, and providing feedback to student responses (Corno & Snow, 1987). Although numerous programs have been developed for observing and improving teacher behaviors, experience indicates that differences in levels of microadaptation will always be present, and that educators and trainers cannot effectively respond to the individual differences represented in groups of students of the size they are expected to instruct as a matter of course.

Computer-Based Adaptive Instructional Systems

Computer-based instruction and controllable learning environments offer the potential for adaptive teaching that is powerful and cost-effective. *Computer-based adaptive instructional systems* are computer programs capable of macroadaptations and microadaptations. The interactive capabilities of computers allow for both long-term planning and the moment-to-moment decisions required for effective adaptation. If a computer is programmed for adaptive teaching, this expertise would be available for other computers and students in the future. In addition, the computer can monitor each and every response and will not become discouraged if students respond poorly. According to Corno and Snow (1987):

> Computerized instruction holds the promise to model systematically *microadaptation* more immediately than do classroom teachers . . . Computerized instruction is thus an important vehicle for effective application of adaptive teaching. (p. 614)

The computer can adapt both the form and content of the ongoing instruction to the characteristics of the learner. However, without effective programming, one-to-one instruction by computers will not necessarily embody effective, adaptive teaching. The computer must be programmed to provide the questions, explanations, examples, counter-examples, practice problems, illustrations, activities, and demonstrations which are specifically needed by the student (Ohlsson, 1987).

Computers require sophisticated programs to achieve effective adaptive teaching. Although present CAI tutoring programs frequently include a management system, sophisticated adaptive and generative systems must be added to all existing computer-based instruction to individualize the instruction for the needs of the student. Yang (1987) indicates that:

> From the viewpoint of individualized instruction, it is true that most existing CAI courseware programs are relatively "dumb". . . While traditional CAI is capable of varying instruction to a certain degree, it is not "intelligent" enough to appropriately tailor instruction to match the needs of individual learners . . . (p. 11)

Several models of computer-based adaptive instruction have been explored by educators and trainers. Tennyson and Park (1984) reviewed research models from mathematics, multiple regression analysis techniques, testing and branching, and Bayesian conditional probability. These computer-based adaptive instructional systems were designed to respond and generate instruction based upon the changing history of the student's responses rather than on a single response. For example, Tennyson and his associates have developed a sophisticated adaptive system called the Minnesota Adaptive Instruction System (Tennyson, Christensen, & Park, 1984). This system uses measurement and monitoring systems at macro- and micro-levels of adaptation.

ICAI writers do not consider these computer-based adaptive instructional system to be exemplary of mainstream ICAI research since the adaptations are based on task selection algorithms and parametric summaries of student behavior (Wenger, 1987; Sleeman & Brown, 1982). Although Tennyson and his associates label their program an "intelligent system," they have not emphasized AI processes and tools in their research. Classic ICAI research on adaptive and "intelligent" systems has required the demonstration of AI programming methods and tools. At present, ICAI research has neglected the significant contribution of computer-based adaptive instructional systems toward achieving "intelligence" in teaching because of the traditional methods and tools involved in development.

Many of the problems of education and training might be solved or made more manageable through computer-based adaptive instructional systems. In addition, educators and trainers need to explore AI concepts, procedures, and tools to better understand learning environments, teaching, expertise, and student learning. A complementary solution is that collaborative efforts extend research on computer-based adaptive instructional systems by creating computer-based learning environments to challenge and motivate individuals to maximize their potential. These computer-based adaptive instructional systems should incorporate the research and best practices from both CAI and ICAI.

INTELLIGENT COMPUTER-ASSISTED INSTRUCTION

Intelligent computer-assisted instruction (ICAI) is an area of research and development from artificial intelligence (AI) which promises to significantly improve education and training. AI approaches to computer-based instruction were referred to as "intelligent" computer-assisted instruction when they emerged to meet the shortcomings identified by AI researchers in traditional computer-assisted instruction (CAI). According to Tennyson and Ferrara (1987):

> By simply adding intelligence to CAI, it was possible to immediately establish a new field of inquiry without the usual years of productivity. With only a few examples of experimental prototype, the field of intelligent computer-assisted instruction (ICAI) was well established by the start of the 1980s. (p. 7)

Will this intelligence promised by AI significantly improve computer-based education and training? Present research and development studies have yet to provide an answer.

ICAI systems use sophisticated techniques from AI, cognitive science, and computer science research to enhance instruction, learning environments, and the transfer of expertise. As defined in AI, the term "intelligent" would indicate existence of competence in problem solving. The vision of a computer-based instruction system capable of solving all the problems related to effective instruction emerges from research and development in ICAI. Kearsley (1987) describes this vision in his book, *AI and Instruction* :

> The dream of ICAI researchers is to provide each student with a computer-based tutor that has all of the qualities of a master teacher. This includes great scope and depth of subject matter expertise, excellent knowledge of teaching techniques, powerful communication skills, and the ability to inspire and motivate students to learn. (p. 158)

The superiority of "intelligent" computer-based instructional programs that understand the knowledge, the student, and teaching methodology is considered a crucial difference between ICAI and traditional CAI. Just as AI systems are designed to solve the challenging
problems of computer science, ICAI systems are designed to solve the
challenging problems of education and training.

At present, research in ICAI has been limited to only a few
domains because of the sophistication required for AI programming
and prototype development. ICAI programs have been developed on
large computer systems, and only a few have been ported to microcomputers or computer networks for daily use in classrooms or
training centers (Kearsley, 1987). These ICAI prototypes have been
developed in mathematics, medicine, science, electronics, equipment
repair, and computer programming. ICAI has been focused only on
these well-formulated areas because of the complexities involved in
AI development. According to Allen and Carter (1988):

> One reason for the relatively slow progress in applying expert systems
> technology to the design of tutoring systems is that tutoring is a compli-
> cated activity that integrates very different types of expertise. Tutoring (as
> opposed to advice or consultation) requires knowledge that extends well
> beyond the subject matter domain in which the student is being assisted.
> The system must know about teaching strategies and about how different
> students learn. (p. 124)

These ICAI prototypes are reviewed favorably by proponents of AI.

Educators and trainers are demonstrating an increasing interest in
ICAI and the use of AI concepts, procedures, and tools. Evidence of
this increased interest in ICAI is represented by the numerous articles
in journals such as *Educational Technology*, the *Journal of Computer-based Instruction*, and the *Journal of Instructional Development*. For example, a special issue of *EducationalTechnology* (May,
1987) focused on education and training research in ICAI and expert
systems development. A citation count in the *Journal of Computer-
based Instruction* shows that AI and cognitive science are emerging

as major topics of interest (Wedman, 1987). Further evidence of increased interest in ICAI by educators and trainers is reflected in the recent development of articulate expert systems for education and training as described in Chapter Four. However, with this new interest from education and training has come criticism and awareness of differences. Tennyson and Ferrara (1987) note that:

> Unlike other fields and disciplines which have taken decades to develop, ICAI, because of contemporary interest in rapid computer generation growth, established a scientific language and method from only a handful of examples, and with only minimal scientific review and criticism. (p. 7)

A critical review by Rosenberg (1987) describes major weaknesses in the instructional approaches used in most classic ICAI programs. One assumption of ICAI researchers appears to be that AI concepts, procedures, and tools always improve teaching and learning. According to Hajovy and Christensen (1987):

> Learning and instruction are much more complex processes than are exhibited in the prototype ICAI systems and, when viewed from an educational perspective, these systems have a rather novice approach to both learning and instruction. (p. 9)

As indicated by O'Neal, Anderson, and Freeman (1986):

> ... none of these ICAI projects has been evaluated in any rigorous fashion. In a sense they have been toy systems for research and demonstration. They have raised a good deal of excitement and enthusiasm about their likelihood of being effective instructional environments. (p. 985)

Educators and trainers must consider these limits and reservations in their review of books and articles by proponents of ICAI systems and in expanding their interaction and experimentation with ICAI systems. To effective evaluate ICAI, a knowledge of its history may prove valuable. A brief history of ICAI and its relationships with CAI and AI is presented in Box 5.1.

Box 5.1

A Brief History of Intelligent CAI

ICAI research and development has emerged to test AI concepts and processes and to meet the perceived needs currently unmet by computer-assisted instruction (CAI). CAI has a relatively long history starting with the teaching machine work of Pressey in 1926 prior to the invention of computers. Initial approaches to CAI development focused on sequences of "frames" (different from the knowledge representation technique) that presented explanatory information and a question. These questions needed to be answered correctly by the learner before proceeding to the next frame. Crowder (1962) used a more sophisticated branching or "scrambled textbook" approach similar to Skinner's programmed instruction materials. Branching to frames or sections was based upon one or a small block of questions.

Computer-based adaptive instructional systems were introduced by Atkinson (1972) to optimize instruction through mathematical models which reduced the probability of student error. Suppes and his associates used trajectory models of multiple regression analysis as an adaptation technique. Work continues by Tennyson and his associates on adaptations based upon testing, measurement, and Bayesian conditional probability (Tennyson, 1987).

The extension of CAI into "generative systems" emphasized the use of algorithms to generate problems and solutions based upon the needs of the learner. Prior to ICAI research efforts beginning in the 1970s, the computers uses in education were dominated by CAI which incorporated programmed instruction and instructional design in its best applications.

Research in intelligent computer-assisted instruction (ICAI) has centered around a series of classic prototypes and issues in cognitive science and AI. ICAI was introduced in an important paper by Carbonell (1970a) which describes both needed changes in CAI design and the major characteristics of

ICAI programs as mixed-initiative dialogue, knowledge representation, student models, diagnostic error rules, and natural language. These characteristics are still critical issues in ICAI research.

ICAI started as a distinct approach with the development of SCHOLAR, a South American geography program, by Carbonell, Collins, and colleagues at Bolt, Beranek, and Newman, Inc., which included these characteristics. SCHOLAR exemplifies a mixed-initiative dialogue system and uses a semantic network of facts and concepts as an extensive data base. The program allows the student to ask questions in a limited natural language. This mixed-initiative dialogue is significantly different from previous linear branching and frame oriented CAI programs.

Knowledge representation has been explored in ICAI development. Early ICAI programs such as SCHOLAR and SOPHIE used semantic networks as the basis for representing knowledge. Later ICAI programs have used production rules of the IF-THEN type to represent knowledge. Recent ICAI efforts have expanded these previous efforts to include object oriented programming and multiple representation approaches.

Expert systems were explored as the knowledge base for an ICAI system called GUIDON. GUIDON was developed by William Clancey in the late 1970s. Clancey (1987) continues his research on ICAI through work on NEOMYCIN, a structural revision of MYCIN, and GUIDON2.

Intelligent simulations or reactive learning environments were explored by ICAI researchers, John Seeley Brown and Richard Burton, in their program SOPHIE. SOPHIE functioned as an automated lab designed around a simulated electrical circuit. Recent research on SOPHIE II and III have focused on articulate experts and differences between human and machine reasoning.

Several other classic prototypes such as STEAMER, BUGGY, and WUSOR are listed in Table 5.1 and used to illustrate the range of ICAI applications later in this chapter.

ICAI and AI

The dominant influence of AI and the minimal influence of education and training have important implications for determining the long-term impact of ICAI. ICAI research and development has been initially a domain of AI, computer science, and cognitive science. The goal of AI has been to create a working prototype which demonstrates intelligence in adaptive teaching. Kearsley (1987) indicates the direction of ICAI development:

> Developers of ICAI systems focus on problems of knowledge representation, student misconceptions, and inferencing. By and large, they have ignored instructional theory and past research findings in computer-based instruction. (p. 1)

ICAI researchers are pursuing AI and cognitive science goals related to finding out how intelligence works rather than education and training goals related to effective and efficient instruction. As noted by Self (1988):

> ICAI researchers, regrettably, perhaps—are more interested in the computational expression of principles of learning and teaching than in the provision of systems for real use in present educational settings. (p. xvi)

Although ICAI experimental prototypes have been demonstrated during the past twenty years, these prototypes have had no real impact on conventional instruction at present.

AI research and development emphasizes the demonstration of AI processes and tools in their working prototypes. Hajovy and Christenson (1987) note that :

> Current ICAI programs are basically prototype systems whose aim is to enhance instruction through the employment of computer-based software tools. Most of these tools are directly associated with the expert systems methods of the artificial intelligence (AI) field. (p. 9)

ICAI prototypes have been constructed by small teams of AI researchers in advanced facilities of major universities or research laboratories. These teams have developed prototype systems in their own areas of expertise and interests such as mathematics and computer programming. Instructional designers, domain experts, educators, and trainers have not been members of these teams. Since most ICAI researchers are responsible for their own programming, ICAI programs have been developed with AI tools and languages on expensive AI purpose hardware or LISP machines. This special hardware is designed for AI research by companies such as Symbolic, Xerox, Texas Instruments, and Lamda (Park & Seidel, 1987). Programming has been primarily in LISP, Prolog, or expert system development tools developed specifically for this hardware. This approach to prototype construction is sufficiently remote from the real demands of education and training to seriously question the impact of ICAI efforts on education and training. Because of the remoteness of the ICAI prototypes from the real demands of education and training settings, education and training specialists have become "skeptical of the practical value of ICAI" (Kearsley, 1987).

Evaluation in ICAI has involved an AI approach to computer-based instructional systems which is different from that followed by education and training. Hofmeister (1986) describes formative and summative procedures of educational research and evaluation which should be implemented by ICAI and expert systems developers. System validation in ICAI has not met research and evaluation criteria established in instructional design. ICAI testing is "poorly controlled, incompletely reported, inconclusive, and in some cases totally lacking" (Rosenberg, 1987). The few prototypes developed in ICAI have not received formative and summative evaluations, and often have been judged to be successful when they met the minimum criterion of running competently. An example of this preoccupation with powerful prototypes which demonstrate a strong single feature is shown by the philosophy of the MIT Media Lab. Its philosophy is "Demo or die," in contrast to traditional research approaches which require testing and publication—"Publish or perish." In contrast to the minimal number of evaluated prototypes of AI, thousands of CAI programs have been developed on low-cost microcomputers and classroom computer networks, and many programs have received extensive formative and summative evaluations.

ICAI and CAI

Computer-assisted instruction (CAI) appears to have only a minimal impact on ICAI at present. Educators and trainers may best understand this limited impact by comparing and contrasting ICAI with the traditional use of computer-assisted instruction (CAI) with which they are likely to be familiar. According to Yang (1987):

> The term "intelligent" in ICAI should be treated as an adjective which describes the ability of an ICAI program rather than as a condition which separates ICAI from other CAI courseware. (p. 12)

However, Park, Perez and Seidel (1987) indicate that at present the differences between ICAI and CAI are more significant than the "I" would indicate. They discuss a long list of differences in goals, theoretical bases, instructional principles, methods of structuring knowledge, instructional formats, subject matter areas, development process, program validation, hardware, software, and terminology. Although some differences are not crucial, educators and trainers should be aware that many of these differences must be eliminated or reduced if ICAI is to be improved.

A consistent criticism of ICAI is that the instructional models and theories used are not fully developed and frequently are limited to a discovery learning approach. In a highly critical article, Rosenberg (1987) discusses models of teaching and learning that are "not well grounded" and based upon "a paucity of pedological theory about tutoring." The theoretical basis of CAI includes learning and instructional theories from programmed instruction and instructional design in contrast to the discovery learning and cognitive development approaches of ICAI. According to Kearsley (1987):

> Researchers who have developed past ICAI programs have tended to be computer scientists rather than specialists in CAI. To a large extent, these researchers have not been fully cognizant of the state of the art in conventional CAI applications, tending to characterize the field as still being stuck in the drill-and-practice, or frame-oriented, tutorials of the sixties. In fact, many current applications of CAI in education and training involve sophisticated simulations, diagnostic testing, and problem-solving sequences. (p. 157)

Most crucially, reviews of ICAI literature reveal that AI researchers have neglected instructional research from education and training.

Fortunately, the relationship between ICAI and traditional CAI is improving. One goal for ICAI is to experiment with AI tools in CAI research and development (Tennyson & Ferrara, 1987). In the future, many ICAI programs may employ AI and expert systems tools while focusing on variables and strategies directly related to instruction and learning (Hajovy & Christensen, 1987). In addition, ICAI researchers are beginning to recognize the importance of teaching research (Clancey, 1987; Woolf, 1987).

Several educators and trainers have suggested that a complementary relationship might be developed between ICAI and CAI (Merrill, 1987; Woodward and Carnine, 1987). According to Lippert (1989)

> It is generally believed that the true forte of ICAI will come in areas were traditional forms of instruction work poorly; transforming enviornments to make them physically safe and economically feasible, to permit exploration at a variety of levels of detail and abstraction, and to allow students to design and carry out novel experiments, learn from mistakes, and suffer the results born from insufficient data. (p.13)

For example, Bonner (1987) proposed that computer courseware be viewed as a continuum with expert systems and intelligent tutoring extending the traditional CAI approaches. In this proposed continuum, ICAI efforts would address problems of education and training which cannot be solved by traditional CAI approaches. For example, some goals and objectives may be met more easily with traditional courseware such as drill and practice. ICAI efforts would only add intelligence to the simple drill and practice approach when required to attain these goals and objectives. The continuum indicates that more complex problems can be solved by sophisticated computer-based instruction systems of ICAI. CAI research would be extended to include an understanding of the student, the learning environment, adaptive teaching, and the specific area of expertise addressed by the proposed instruction.

TYPES OF ICAI SYSTEMS

ICAI may be divided into different categories to show the range of teaching and learning models being explored by AI researchers. Lawler and Yazdani (1987) divide ICAI into the two general approaches of intelligent tutoring systems (ITS) and computer-based learning environments. Kearsley (1987) divides ICAI into five categories (1) articulate expert systems, (2) mixed initiative dialogues, (3) diagnostic tutors, (4) computer coaches, and (5) microworlds. The classification system of Lawler and Yazdani (1987) is not incompatible with that of Kearsley (1987) since mixed-initiative dialogues and diagnostic tutors may be viewed as subcategories of ITS and microworlds are a subcategory of computer-based learning environments. Articulate expert systems and coaches may be classified either as components of ITS or as consultants in an intelligent learning environment. In real world applications of ICAI, all types may be linked into hybrid programs. Figure 5. 1 shows a classification system for ICAI applications which clarifies the relationship between Lawler and Yazdani (1987) and Kearsley (1987).

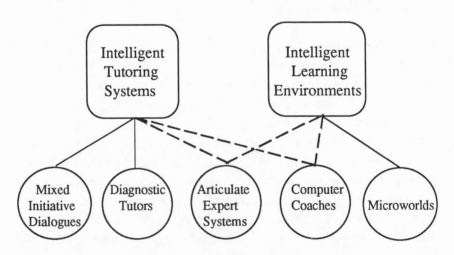

FIGURE 5.1
Classification System
for ICAI Applications

Intelligent Tutoring Systems

The term "intelligent tutoring systems" (ITS) is sometimes used as an equivalent term to ICAI. In fact, many AI researchers greatly prefer this term and the abbreviation ITS since it indicates an approach that is clearly differentiated from CAI (Wenger, 1987). However, the terms are not interchangeable, ITS is only one area of ICAI and emphasizes only one instructional strategy—tutoring (Knezek, 1988). Tutoring is a type of instructional dialogue which presents material to the student, asks questions of the student, and provides feedback and remedial material when appropriate. Some educators believe that the "wide-spread adoption of the term ITS is "unfortunate" (Merrill, 1987). Tutorials are not an "ideal" or "universal" teaching strategy, but merely one type of strategy which has limited purposes. For example, tutorials might be used to remediate problems or to clarify concepts during a simulation activity. Merrill (1987) indicates that the term "tutoring" is overused in ICAI research and limits computer-based instruction by not including simulations, learning environments, and expanded teaching functions.

"Intelligent" tutoring focuses on improving communication and remediation based upon an understanding of the student's responses to questions. Herbert A. Simon (1969) summarized the role of a "good" tutor by stating that:

> . . . a "good" tutor plays the role of a knowledgeable friend who only suggests and advises, leaving the control of the learning situation essentially in the hands of the student. (p.115)

Thus, the role of the ITS program is to react only after the student has erred on the way to solving the problem at hand. The reaction to the program is to be diagnostic in the sense that the program analyzes the pattern of student errors and advises the student regarding solutions or solution strategies that will put the student back on track. Classic ITS research primarily explores the mixed-initiative dialogue, diagnotic tutors, and computer coaches. Table 5.1 presents a listing of ITS programs and their content areas, knowledge representation techniques, types, and primary references.

TABLE 5.1
Intelligent Tutoring Systems

Program	Content	Knowledge Representation	Type	References
SCHOLAR	Geography	Semantic Network	Dialogue	Carbonell, 1970
WHY	Cause of rainfall	Scripts	Dialogue	Stevens & Collins, 1977
SOPHIE	Electronic repair	Semantic Net/ Simulator	Simulation	Brown & Burton, 1975
STEAMER	Steamship propulsion	Procedural/ Simulator	Simulation	Hollan, Hutchins, & Weitzman, 1987
EXCHECK	Logic and set theory	Rule-based	Reactive environment	Suppes, 1981
WEST	Arithmetic	Rule-based	Coach	Burton & Brown, 1979
WUSOR	Logic	Semantic Network	Coach	Carr & Goldstein, 1977
DEBUGGY	Subtraction	Procedural	Diagnostic Tutor	Burton & Brown, 1978
LMS	Algebra	Rule-based	Diagnostic Tutor	Sleeman, 1982
PROUST	Pascal programming	Semantic Network	Reactive Environment	Johnson & Soloway, 1985
GUIDON	Medical diagnosis	Rule-based	Dialogue	Clancey, 1982
ACTP	Geometry/ LISP	Rule-based	Tutor	Anderson, 1983

Mixed-Initiative Dialogues. Some ITS programs teach by engaging the student in a conversation and tutor the student via a Socratic method of guided discovery. Mixed-initiative dialogues have the capability of allowing students to ask questions of the ITS program rather than the conventional program initiated questions and information presentations of traditional CAI tutoring. The optimal result of this two-way interaction would be a dialogue or conversation between the student and a knowledgeable teacher. Mixed-initiative dialogues were the original type of ITS program. GUIDON has limited mixed-initiative dialogue capabilities.

Diagnostic Tutors. ITS programs often emphasize the identification and correction of student errors and misconceptions (Kearsley, 1987). The learner is placed in a tutoring situation and allowed to make errors. Some diagnostic tutors have a catalog of student "bugs" or conceptual errors. This type of ITS is appropriate for any problem solving situation where instructional prescriptions can be generated by identifying and analyzing students' patterns of errors. Diagnostic tutors engage the student in a simulation or a game, as well as tutoring; and then react to the student's errors or questions. Diagnostic tutors attempt to guide students through the process of debugging their own misconceptions. Box 5.2 describes the classic ITS prototypes BUGGY and DEBUGGY as examples of a diagnostic tutors.

Computer Coaches. Like human coaches, computer coaches guide the student during a game or simulation while monitoring the student's performance. These coaches provide advice to help the student improve his or her performance. The major issue for coaching programs are when to interrupt the student and what advice to give. Coaches will complement microworlds and other learning environments by adding intelligent monitoring and assistance. Box 5.3 illustrates computerized coaching with a description of the classic computer coaching prototype, WUSOR.

Box 5.2
BUGGY and DEBUGGY—Diagnostic Tutors

BUGGY and DEBUGGY are classic ICAI programs which continue to impact research on diagnostic tutors. BUGGY is a game for teacher trainees in which they are encouraged to discover "bugs" or procedural errors through an analysis of student solutions to place-value subtraction problems. The purpose of BUGGY is to train student teachers in the recognition of student problems in subtraction. In the development of BUGGY, Brown and Burton (1978) analyzed the protocols of hundreds of students to determine not only the correct procedural subskills, but also the possible "bugs." The term "bug" is adopted from computer science to describe internalized incorrect procedures which students use in solving a range of problems.

DEBUGGY is a diagnostic system which extends the BUGGY research by analyzing tests taken by students to determine their procedural "bugs." An on-line version called IDEBUGGY "incrementally" presents students with new problems to solve in an effort to diagnosis the causes of difficulties in subtraction. DEBUGGY demonstrates the feasibility and complexity of using a catalog of bugs to develop a diagnostic system. The work of the project has been continued with the development of REPAIR and STEP theories to assist students in correcting errors.

The assumption of the diagnostic research of this project is that mistakes are the result of learned incorrect procedures rather than the inability to follow the correct procedures presented by the teacher. Although a catalog of procedural errors were identified through this long-term project in the limited procedural area of place-value subtraction, diagnositic systems in complex and nonprocedural domain may not be possible. However, many domains of education and training might be open to diagnostic tutors.

Box 5.3

WUMPUS and WUSOR—Computer Coaches

The WUSOR project was developed to explore issues in computer coaching for the computer game WUMPUS. This computer game challenges the player to shoot the dangerous Wumpus while avoiding the dangers of pits, bats and the Wumpus. The player moves throughout the caves and receives warnings such as drafts from the pits, squeaks from the bats, and the stench of the Wumpus. The player must use logic and probability to win the game.

Three generations of WUSOR have been developed to demonstrate aspects of computer coaching in this limited domain of WUMPUS game expertise. A modular approach to development was used with the Expert, Psychologist, Tutor, and Student each serving separate roles. For example, the Expert uses rules representing the expertise necessary to play the game effectively. The Expert informs the Psychologist if the players moves are nonoptimal. The Psychologist acts as a diagnositician who identifies student error patterns. The Tutor uses rules to determine when appropriate topics should be discussed with the player. The Student is an overlay model of the Expert which indicates rules which have been learned and the level of play. This modular approach allowed project developers to focus on differing aspects of computer coaching.

Overlay models may be used when domain expertise is expressed as a set of rules. The student's knowledge is then stored as a subset of the the expert's knowledge, thus the term "overlay." The WUSOR projects explored the domain expertise required for computer coaches. A major finding is the critical importance of capturing the domain expertise prior to the development of ICAI systems. Research on computer coaches continues in areas of diagnosis, tutoring, and learning environments.

Intelligent Learning Environments

Intelligent learning environments include microworlds, simulations, and multimedia environments for learning. The purpose of computer-based learning environments is to allow students to manipulate concepts and processes. *Learning environment* may be broadly defined to include a wide range of experiential uses of the computer. For example, Merrill (1988) notes that:

> The computer is not a single medium but a multimedia device. Rather than a single metaphor (tutoring) it is possible to think of many metaphors to represent the various interactions that are possible. In addition to a participant in a conversation where there is give and take, the computer can be a laboratory where the student can manipulate devices, change data, observe reactions and test hypotheses. The computer can be a blueprint or a circuit diagram which the student can design or change. The computer is a drawing table where the student can illustrate his/her ideas and have them critiqued. The computer is word processor which enables the student to edit material and have this material monitored. The computer is a calculator, a control panel, a machine, or any of a hundred devices to be manipulated. To limit the metaphor for instruction to the computer as tutor is to limit the nature of instruction. (p. 9)

Intelligent learning environments must include the capabilities of monitoring and guiding students as they interact with the simulation, microworld, or empowering environment for learning. Intelligent learning environments should be capable of demonstrating how the concepts and processes within the world work, explaining the underlying principles, and detect student errors. Unless connected to intelligent tutors, coaches, or expert systems, these "instructionally oriented symbolic manipulation tools" are passive and reactive (Dede, 1986). Some reviews of ICAI do not include learning environments as a type of ICAI system since most are passive environments without additional "intelligent" subsystems. Research and development in learning environments such as LOGO and inspectable simulations such as STEAMER have not included these features. The following complementary types of intelligent learning environments have the potential of empowering students and trainees: microworlds, simulations, and hypermedia environments.

Microworlds. Microworlds are computer-programming environments for experimenting with concepts, and procedures. Microworlds may be created at various levels of complexity appropriate for the learner. For example, microworlds created for an expert would be at a higher level of abstraction than those created for the novice or an intermediate student. Most interactions with microworlds involve student controlled discovery and explorations. However, discovery and exploration are a limited form of interaction which may require direct instruction, monitoring and guidance for optimal learning.

Microworlds may be illustrated by a range of examples. The LOGO programming language is the best known example of a microworld in education. LOGO is a microworld and simple programming language which allows children to create "turtle" graphics and explore concepts in geometry. The use of microworlds in areas such as mathematics and music continues to receive a great deal of attention in education. Box 5.4 describes other examples of microworlds for children. Individuals of all ages can use microworlds such as artificial oceans, ecosystems, and power plants to allow the trainee to explore and change aspects of these learning environments. The present use of the term "microworlds" by ICAI researchers encompasses many types of simulation.

Simulations. Simulations are any type of computer-based learning which seeks to imitate aspects of the real world. Simulations are devices, computer programs, or mulitmedia environments that model a real system or situation. Computer-based simulations are capable of recreating procedures, processes, and causal relationships encountered during real life situations. These simulations provide important learning environments which have the potential for instructional components to optimize and transfer learning.

Simulation is a pervasive area of computer-based learning with many examples presently being used in both education and training. Examples range widely from serious training applications in business, military, and industry to fun activities in education and recreation. Simulations vary from simplistic decision models with few choices to dynamic models which encompass all choices required for realism.

Box 5.4
Microworlds for Children

Microworlds present exciting possibilities for motivating children. These computer-based learning environments provide limitless possibilities for experimentation and problem solving. Some of these possibilities are shown by the well-known microworld–LOGO and recent extension such as mathematical microworlds of LEGO and MOTIONS. However, more obvious examples may be found in our own homes and the videogame centers.

Several examples of motivating computer-based environments can be selected from the wide range of videogames now available on specially designed game machines by companies such as Nintendo and Atari. Although educators might question the value of problem solving and psychomotor skills required, commercial sales and informal observations of children and youth engaged in using these programs confirm the high state motivation generated by these videogame environments or microworlds. This motivation seems to be superior to that provide by microworlds such as LOGO or present CAI programs.

The range of videogames now available is equally impressive. For example, sports games include basketball, football, golf, tennis, boxing, karate, volleyball, hockey, and others. The adventure games range from fantasy to various war and combat games. Some fantasy games use the "worlds" concept with characters traveling through several different kinds of worlds and levels to win or master the game.

From an educational perspective, it is difficult to determine the goals or objectives that learners achieve as they win a computer-based sport or complete levels and worlds in an adventure game. From a time on task perspective, these videogames are either wonderful or dangerous. Most children and youths will spend immense amounts of time playing these games, unless that time is limited by an adult. Obviously, the developers of these games have not been concerned with educational goals and objectives at present. Their primary motivation would appear to be the number of programs sold.

An exciting example of future microworlds is provided by AI researcher, Alan Kay, in his project called "Vivarium." Vivarium is a long-term project of the MIT Media Lab and Apple Computer to develop an exciting learning environment for children. Vivarium exemplifies a challenging area of collaborative research. According to Kay, founder of the project:

> In order to work, the Vivarium needs new kinds of animation and robotics, new kinds of artificial intelligence and computer modeling, new kinds of interface with the user, and possibly a whole new computer "architecture." It also needs fresh insights into neurophysiology, animal behavior, ecology, and experimental education. (Quoted in Brand, 1988, p. 99)

Vivarium means an enclosed environment for life (Brand, 1988). The Vivarium project involves the development of an aquarium-like environment that children can use to create, control, and manipulate animals. In addition, these highly realistic animals would behave and adapt on their own based upon their selected characteristics in the computerized ecosystem. Activities which allow the creation and observations of life are designed to motivate children to learn about science and ecological systems.

One aspect of the Vivarium project is research on friendly and unique interface systems. Children will be able to select characteristics using a large puppet called Noobie as a computer interface. The squeezing or touching of sensors in areas like the hands, ears, and mouth would place a menu of features on the monitor in Noobie's belly. The child could create a creature through this selection process rather than by using a less-friendly keyboard. This prototype projected should lead to a better understanding of many aspects of intelligent learning environments.

Hypermedia Environments. Computer graphics or devices such as videodisc players provide a "visually rich" and "informationally dense" world for exploration (Woolf, 1987). Hypermedia environments allow for the seamless linkage of media or multimedia devices such as the computer, videodisc, CD-ROM players, and other devices. The term "hypermedia" is a synthesis of the instructional technology term "multimedia" and the AI term "hypertext." *Multimedia* is a combination of audio and visual media that is integrated into a structured and systematic presentation (Heinich, Molenda, & Russell, 1985). *Hypertext* is defined by the coiner Theodor Nelson (1988) as "non-sequential writing where the user may move free." Hypermedia extends the concept "hypertext" to include graphic and animation as well as other interactive systems such as videodisc and CD-ROM. The unique interactive features of hypermedia provide high potential for replacing printed materials as a knowledge and information delivery system for many purposes.

Hypertext has been an area of informational science research for twenty years. Nelson (1988) describes his present vision of hypertext and hypermedia:

> ... a world in which everything that is published becomes electronically available, in an ever-growing interconnected whole. Imagine the millions of books and magazines that are now on paper, all the published photographs and paintings and sheet music, now cross-connected in many directions, and all available at once through your screen ... Universal or grand hypertext, then, means a new publishing system—an accessible great universe of linked documents and graphics (and audio recordings and video and movies). (p. 5)

Some indicators of the emergence of interest in the concept of hypermedia is the recent publication such as a magazine called *HyperAge—The Journal of HyperThinking,* a special issue on hypermedia in *Educational Technology* (November 1988), and a recent book titled *Hypertext/Hypermedia* (Jonassen, 1989). Media devices for mass storage of information increase the potential of hypermedia in education and training.

Laser videodiscs are a promising technology for the delivery of hypermedia in education and training. Research on interactive videodiscs has demonstrated their effectiveness and contributions in several areas of health, defense, industrial training, and public school education . Laser videodisc systems are superior to videotape media in rapid and precise access to frames, unlimited still frame capability, greater storage density, and virtual indestructibility of discs (Iuppa, 1984). Random access in under three seconds allows for easy retrieval of any sequence or frame of information. With effective design, level three interactive videodiscs which combine microcomputers and videodisc players can achieve training effectiveness through demonstration, adaptability, feedback on consequences of decisions, and consistency of instruction (Daynes & Butler, 1984; DeBloois, 1982; DeBloois, 1985). With their high capacity storage and their interactive capabilities, laser videodiscs are an ideal media device for development of intelligent learning environments. According to Allen and Carter (1988):

> Interactive videodisc technology provides powerful representational capabilities for tutoring activities. An interactive video system can be thought of as a bundle of independently controllable subsystems:
> videodisc images;
> audio channel 1;
> audio channel 2;
> computer-generated text;
> computer-generated graphics. (p. 127)

These capabilities may be used by ICAI developers to create intelligent learning environments or ITS programs.

Compact Disc-Read Only Memory (CD-ROM) is another media device which is increasingly being used as a storage device for hypermedia. At present, materials such as the encyclopedia, dictionary, ERIC resources and other similar references have been ported to CD-ROM for access and retreival. In the future, CD-ROM discs may be used to store interactive simulations, microworlds, and other learning environments (Miller, 1987).

COMPONENTS OF ICAI

ICAI uses a component or modular approach to development. The interaction among components must be designed so they work together during the process of adaptive teaching (Dede, 1986). The following are potential components of an ICAI system:

1. Simulation module,
2. Expertise module,
3. Teaching module, and
4. Student module.

Each module can be developed and evaluated separately from other modules. The long-term goal of ICAI projects should be to have effective modules which work together to produce an effective teaching or training system.

A modular approach to ICAI development has several advantages over computer-based instruction approaches that integrate content and instruction. Separate ICAI modules provide opportunities for research on areas such as student characteristics (student module), teaching effectiveness (teaching module), clarity of the knowledge base (expertise module), and learning environments (simulation module). The flexibility of modular development will allow educators and trainers to adopt one or all of the ICAI components since each can be evaluated and revised separately from the others (Roberts & Park, 1983).

A significant difference between ICAI and CAI is in the structural organization of the programs. Traditional CAI is "statically" organized while ICAI has "dynamic" access to knowledge. Wenger (1987) uses the analogy of book production to describe the static organization of traditional CAI programs. For example, books and traditional CAI accommodate levels of differential use by allowing students to skip of topics and segments. However, a weakness of books and traditional CAI is that they combine the knowledge of the content, communication, and production in one component. In contrast, ICAI is modular. By capturing expertise in each separate area of modeling, ICAI programs should be able to respond dynamically to situations and decision making.

Simulation Module

The simulation module is the component of an ICAI system that allows the student or trainee to explore real world applications. A simulation module can be developed so that the students or trainees can manipulate variables in the learning environment and observe the concrete models produced to better understand the processes, causes, or procedures. A senario of real life situations or an imitation of real world objects may be recreated in the simulation module. A model of the situation allows the computer to respond to the learner's actions.

Simulation modules are important because they provide a link to exploratory learning environments. According to Lawler and Yazdani (1987):

> The essential strength of such exploratory learning environments is that they can provide individuals with simple, concrete models of important things, ideas, and their relationships. (p. x)

These simulations may be used to reduce costs or to provide safety which would not be possible in a real world experiment. Repeated use of the simulation module will allow the student and trainee to observe and test hypotheses during their experiements. According to Reigeluth and Schwartz (1988):

> Computer-based simulations can provide efficient, effective, and highly motivational instruction that can readily serve the need for individualization. Simulations also enhance the tranfer of learning by teaching complex tasks in an environment that approximates the real world in certain ways. (p. 1)

The simulation module requires other modules to optimize adaptive teaching. In traditional CAI, simulation provides an experimental environment, but without monitoring and guidance. STEAMER, an important ICAI research prototype, is "an inspectable, simulation-based training system" which is presently exploring the relationship between the simulation and other modules (Hollan, Hutchins, & Weitzman, 1987). Box 5.5 further describes the STEAMER project.

Box 5.5

STEAMER—An Interactive Inspectable Simulation

STEAMER provides an exploratory learning environment for military training. STEAMER is an interactive, inspectable simulation which was developed to train engineers in the operation of a steam propulsion system. An interactive and inspectable simulation allows the trainee to control, manipulate, and monitor a dynamic physical system. This simulation provides the trainee with an operating model of the steam propulsion plant which allows the trainee to perform procedures of operation during normal and abnormal conditions. STEAMER is not a toy system, but a high-fidelity simulator which is used in Naval training. The principal investigators in the STEAMER project were James Hollan and Mike Williams from the Naval Personnel and Development Center, and Albert Stevens, Bruce Roberts, and Ken Forbus from Bolt, Beranek and Newman (BBN). This training project is an AI and cognitive science research and development effort.

A major purpose of the cognitive science research related to STEAMER is the development of an understanding of mental models. Mental models are abstractions used by experts to understand how a dynamic physical system works. Mental models do not reflect the exact physical model, but instead attempt to capture the expert's understanding of procedures of operation. Conceptual fidelity emphasizes the concepts and reasoning about the physical system. It reflects the expert's understanding of principles and core concepts required for operation. Operating the simulated plant allows the trainee to learn procedures and to form a sophisticated mental model of the plant's operation. STEAMER research attempts to determine how trainees might be supported during the development of the mental models needed to reason about the steam propulsion system. Computer graphic approximations of the expert's models are used to show the mental models to the trainee.

AI and computer science researchers are studying the impact of graphic interfaces on training. The graphic interface of STEAMER allows the trainee to view and manipulate the power plant at different levels. The computer graphics display allows trainees to view and explore the system and subsystems in further detail. A major emphasis of STEAMER research is the interative exploration of graphic interfaces to simulate physical systems (Hollan, Hutchins, & Weitzman, 1987). Control of the simulation is made possible by multiple windows. The views range between abstract representation of the basic steam cycle to concrete views of gauges panels and subsystems.

Research continues on the teaching and student modules of the STEAMER project. Tutorial and explanatory facilities have been added to improve the training capabilities. The feedback minilab module allows the trainee to explore the structure of specific components by assembling and testing simulated devices. The interactive simulation creates the possibility of different types of instructional interactions. The levels of inspectability allow for an understanding of the processes in the steam propulsion system which normally requires years of instruction and experience before expert operator status is achieved. Recent research on graphic authoring systems has been inspired by STEAMER research and development (Williams, Hollan, & Stevens, 1983).

Other AI research and development projects are using the success of the STEAMER prototype to explore other areas of training. For example, Woolf, Blegen, and Jansen (1986) describe an interactive simulation with helps, hints, explanations, and tutoring to teach a complex industrial process. This project replicates STEAMER research in training novices in the control of recovery boilers for the American Paper Institute. This prototype has been beta tested in pulp and paper mills throughout the United States.

Expertise Module

The expertise module is the component of the ICAI system that contains the declarative, procedural, and heuristic knowledge of the domain expert. Declarative knowledge includes concepts and relationships required for solution of the problems. Procedural knowledge includes step by step procedures used by the domain expert. Heuristic knowledge is the actions and rules which capture the expert's experience related to solving the specific problems. According to Wenger (1987), the expertise module:

> . . . contains a representation of the knowledge to be communciated. In most cases, this representation of the subject matter is not only a description of the various concepts and skills the student is to acquire, as in a curriculum, but an actual model, which can perform in the domain and thus provide the system with a dynamic form of expertise. (p. 14)

The expertise module has many purposes. Dede (1986) describes the functions of the expertise module:

> An ICAI expertise module, while necessarily narrow in its content domain, serves a variety of functions. Educational applications demand a knowledge representation which facilitates access, reasoning, planning, problem solving, pattern recognition, communication, acquisition/expansion, hypothesis generation/evaluation and question answering. (p. 332)

This expertise module can and should work independently of the ICAI system as an articulate expert system. The expertise module must be able to solve the problems presented to the student and arbitrary examples chosen by the student. This problem solving capability should be transparent or a "glass box" to the student or trainee.

The expertise module influences the development of the teaching and student modules, and so development of the expertise module should be developed and evaluated prior to its use in an ICAI system. This expertise module acts as both the source for the expertise, and in addition determines solution path standard for evaluating the student's performance. This standard is used by the teaching module and student module to provide information for computer-based adaptive teaching.

Teaching Module

The teaching module captures the expertise of a model educator or trainer and uses it to determine when and how to teach and communicate with the learner. Teaching knowledge is a separate domain of expertise in ICAI, which is accumulated and codified to guide effective and adaptive teaching. Dialogue management and communication knowledge are skills that a teaching module must possess. This module must be able to motivate students to seek and apply knowledge. The teaching module must know how to select problems or cases which are appropriate to the student's level of understanding and chooses appropriate examples (and non-examples). In addition, the teaching module must be able to review previously learned materials. Teaching or pedagogical knowledge becomes a "second knowledge base" which can be combined with other ICAI modules.

ICAI reseach and development has been only minimally concerned with how to teach effectively. The teaching module is the least studied of the ICAI components (Clancey, 1987). A critical need of ICAI research is the development of an expert teaching model which reflects the findings of teaching research and best individualized instruction practices. Teaching knowledge must clarify and codify many of the individualized teaching behaviors of an expert teacher. A knowledge engineering approach to building an expert teaching model would be to identify the knowledge base used by educators and trainers during effective individualized instruction. References to instruction or the expert teaching model in the AI literature have been general and focus mainly on program control and knowledge communications. Classic ICAI programs have failed to use instructional design approaches or systematic teaching. Rather than assuming that this knowledge base of pedagogy does not exist, ICAI researchers should examine research findings and best practices of education and training to determine how the events of effective instruction can be clarified and codified.

Currently the state of the art in ICAI uses a form of instruction that may be somewhat analagous to conventional and spontaneous teaching techniques, rather that the systematic approach required for effective individualized instruction. If an expert teaching model is to be effectively implemented, the discovery learning assumptions of previous ICAI studies   must be challenged.   Previously developed teaching modules have only explored limited teaching and control options such as when to assist or intervene with a student. These teaching modules simply provide feedback to the student by attempting to say just the right thing so that the student will recognize his or her error and change to the correct response and understand. Barr and Clancey (1982) indicate, however, that "it is by no means clear how *just the right thing* is to be said to the student." In many situations, this reliance upon reactive or discovery learning approaches appears inefficient at best.

Education and training research provides a range of teaching options from direct instruction to discovery learning. There is ". . . a small but well established knowledge base" in education and psychology that firmly supports a more proactive approach to instruction (Brody & Good, 1986). Research has demonstrated that proactive approaches such as modeling and clear demonstrations reduce student error rates and improve student achievement scores. Systematic approaches to instruction which use clear communication to model and lead the students have demonstrated effectiveness in educational research.

Teaching research has strongly questioned the value of high student error rates. Education and training research indicates that student must experience a constant stream of success (Block, 1980). This obviously flies in the face of the ICAI researchers' position advocating the necessity of "floundering." In most classic ICAI programs, students are allowed to "flounder" on the assumption that floundering is a valuable learning experience related to discovery learning. Sleeman and Brown (1982) support the notion of student control in ICAI and extend it to the point that students should even be allowed to "flounder" awhile before being advised. The act of floundering can be "vitally important" they contend.   The direct instruction approach, which allows no such pattern of error on the part of students, provides teaching programs which consistently produce substantial progress. ICAI currently allows a great deal of student directed learning and struggle with the concepts and problems. In the process, students are allowed, even expected and perhaps encouraged, to make errors so that the "tutor" can prescribe a course of action based upon the errors. Although the current ICAI systems may be appropriate for some sophisticated learners and for learners who have undergone initial instruction, they are ineffective for many naive learners.

AI research and development will complement present efforts in adaptive teaching research. As noted by Clancey (1987):

> ... the thought lingers that AI has something unique to offer to instruction. We must always be careful of limiting our sights to automating what teachers already do or simply trying to improve upon what they do. (p. 247)

According to Dede (1986):

> Traditional educational research, with its focus on group training, has not supplied an adequate theoretical framework for optimizing individual learning in information-rich environments, so an increased emphasis in ICAI on explanatory strategies is vital. (p. 344)

Educators and trainers should carefully evaluate the findings of ICAI prototype research and development. These findings result from a focus on student modeling and a limitied emphasis on instruction. Most ICAI programs are presently designed to explore student control and modeling. Becker and Carnine (1980) state the importance of effective instruction:

> ...there can be no question that smart adults can organize and sequence experiences which will teach concepts and problem-solving skills better than children. (p. 449)

New ICAI programs must recognize the importance of instructional research and place greater emphasis on the teaching module.

Student Module

The student module develops a model of the learner and uses this student model to make predictions about student misconceptions and learning problems so that the system can track them, identify causes, and suggest corrections. According to Wenger (1987):

> No intelligent communication can take place without a certain understanding of the recipient. Thus, along with the idea of explicitly representing the knowledge to be conveyed came the idea of doing the same with the student, in the form of a student model. Ideally, this model should include all the aspects of the student's behavior and knowledge that have repercussions for his performance and learning. (p. 16)

The student module establishes knowledge of the student which must be updated throughout his or her interactions with the program. The program must first establish whether the student has the prerequisite skills to interact appropriately with the program. The student module is used to assess the student's knowledge in the area of problem solving and to hypothesize about the student's conceptions and reasoning. The student module works with the expertise and teaching modules to model and monitor the student.

AI and cognitive science research has explored student modeling as a major area of educational applications. Student modeling research explores effective methods for monitoring, testing, diagnosing, and remediating student progress. An extensive body of ICAI research has focused on the student module. In addition, education and training research has contributed numerous studies in the area of evaluation and student monitoring. If research from these disciplines can be merged, the student module will be significantly improved.

The complexity of representing important knowledge of the student has resulted in different approaches to student modeling. Each of the approaches to student modeling offers the promise of predicting learner behaviors and diagnosing the cause of student error. Some computer-based adaptive systems use parametic models of the student to predict behaviors. Other student modules monitor the student's knowledge through simple pattern matching and recognition that "flags" the subject-matter facts or rules that the student has mastered. The student module uses the procedures of recording student knowledge mastered and applying pattern recognition to this response history to infer the skills and reasoning used and needed by the student. Clancey (1982) identifies performance progress, direct questions, assumptions about the student's learning experiences, and assumptions about the difficulty of the content of the materials as major sources of information for the student module.The assumption of many student models is that student errors reflect misconceptions about facts and rules, rather than failure to recognize their applicability at appropriate points in the instructional sequence.

The types of Intelligent Tutoring Systems (ITS) influence the approaches to student modeling. For example, most computer coaches represent the student's knowledge as a subset of the expert's knowledge by contrasting the knowledge base of the student to the knowledge base of the expertise module on the same task or problem. This "overlay model" approach to the student module has been developed by Carr and Goldstein (1977). Diagnostic tutors approach student modeling through the "buggy model" which tries to identify rules and "mal-rules" or misconceptions that the student attempts to use in the problem solving process. This diagnostic tutoring approach to student modeling is described by Brown and Burton (1978). These different approaches to student modeling are all being explored to improve computer coaches and tutors.

In the future, the research on the student module will combine with improvements in each of the other modules to create effective computer-based adaptive systems which demonstrate the intelligence of human tutors. In addition, simulation capabilities and multimedia enhancements will provide unique computer-based learning environments with intelligent monitoring and guidance systems.

CHAPTER SUMMARY

• Adaptive teaching and individualized instruction are critical areas of research in education and training. Unfortunately, many of the findings from research on adaptive teaching are stored passively in books or in the minds of expert teachers. If this expertise and knowledge could be effectively used or communicated then teaching would be significantly improved. Computer-based adaptive instructional systems demonstrate capabilities in the area of macroadaptation—curriculum and program level decisions—and in microadaptations—moment-to-moment systematic instruction.

• Intelligent computer-assisted instruction (ICAI) is an AI research and development effort to improve one-to-one instruction through the development of computer-based instruction programs using AI techniques. Major differences exist between ICAI and traditional computer-assisted instruction (CAI) at the present time. These differences must be reduced if ICAI is to significantly impact education and training

• Two general categories of ICAI are intelligent tutoring systems (ITS) and intelligent learning environments. ITS research seeks to develop computer-based instruction systems which teach through mixed-initiative dialogues, diagnostic tutoring, and computer coaching. Intelligent learning environments include a wide range of experiential uses of the computer such as microworlds, simulations, and hypermedia environments.

• The components of an ICAI program are the simulation module, expertise module, student module, and teaching module. The advantage of this modular approach to ICAI is that research and development may focus on one or more of these separate modules. However, the long-term goal of ICAI research is to integrate these modules into effective and computer-based adaptive teaching systems.

• The simulation module allows the student to explore real world applications. A simulation module is linked with other ICAI components to allow the student to manipulate variables in the learning environment and observe the concrete model of an object or situation.

• The expertise module contains the declarative, procedural, and heuristic knowledge. The expertise module can be developed separately as an articulate expert system. The expertise module must be able to solve the problems in the domain. An expertise module is the source for the expertise and a standard for evaluating the student's performance.

• The teaching module is the domain of expertise which guides effective and adaptive teaching. Dialogue management and communciation knowledge are necessary for an effective teaching module. Research in individualized instruction is required for an effective teaching module.

• The student module is used to model the student's performance, predict student misconceptions, and suggest corrections. Student modeling is a major area of ICAI research and prototype development. Overlay models represent the student as a subset of the expert's knowledge as modeled by the expertise module. The buggy model identifies rules and mal-rules which the student uses in problem solving.

SCORECARD				
Will AI Research and Development Efforts Contribute to Education and Training?				
Topics	Question Dimensions			
	Feasibility	Improved Effectiveness	Capacity Enhancing	Future Utility
Adaptive Teaching				
Computer-Based Adaptive Instruction				
Intelligent-Computer Assisted Instruction				
Intelligent Tutoring Systems				
Intelligent Learning Environments				
Simulation Module				
Expertise Module				
Teaching Module				
Student Module				

Comments:

Directions

Imagine an intelligent computer-based adaptive teaching system. Hardware includes a powerful computer, videodisc storage, and high-resolution television. The teaching and learning environment is used by a small cooperative learning group, but each individual must respond to special challenges on his or her own input devices. Each individual plays a role in the simulation. The video program shows scenes based upon the responses. The computer provides knowledge about continuously changing conditions as each learner makes real-time choices. The results of choices are shown both in additional scenes and new information and knowledge. As the interactions continue, a computer-based management system monitors the student and adapts to the individualized needs and goals for each learner. The total impact is an ICAI program that is adaptive, challenging, and creative.

When new technologies such as computer-based teaching have emerged, some educators and trainers have assumed that they have little knowledge to contribute to development and evaluation. At the same time, these educational technologies have failed to significantly alter or advance education and training. Educators and trainers should note that the critical contribution of ICAI is not a breakthough in the field of teaching and learning, but rather in the development of new concepts, processes, and tools which must be used to improve the understanding and application of teaching and learning processes. Some educators and trainers are beginning to realize that their understandings of teaching and learning are critical to effective research, development, and implementation. We perceive both research in computer-based adaptive instructional systems and ICAI to be capacity enhancing with excellent future utility. As educators and trainers, we have found that previously acquired knowledge of teaching and learning is a crucial guide to evaluation of instructional alternatives and emerging technologies.

ICAI is a promising area for teaching and learning research. The effectiveness of ICAI research findings should be determined by monitoring instructional and learning effectiveness and efficiency. The modularity and adaptability of ICAI systems should be extended to all computer-based instructional systems so that inclusion of research and best practice in the development of each module can be undertaken independently. Although ICAI has received some positive attention from experts in education and training journals and magazines, the effectiveness of ICAI prototypes has not been demonstrated by research findings. Computers are not presently adaptive or intelligent enough to outperform human tutors. Therefore, research on effective teaching and learning is required to improve both human and computerized teaching. Unfortunately, this potential has not yet been fulfilled because the understanding of how people learn and how they solve problems is extremely complex, and research efforts in teaching and computer technology are mostly inadequate for the development of computer-based instruction which will enable effective individualization. This fact underlies the importance of educators and trainers pursuing interaction with ICAI researchers and the importance of using and improving knowledge engineering techniques to more efficiently and effectively capture and portray expertise.

ICAI programs should be developed in education and training to solve real-world problems. Although many strengths have emerged from AI and ICAI research, educators and trainers must continue to be aware of the limited impact of ICAI research in education and training settings. Educators and trainers should not assume AI approaches to CAI are superior to traditional approaches unless the instructional programs have demonstrated effectiveness in classrooms and training centers against the same criteria used in the summative evaluation phase of instructional design processes. Some ICAI prototypes such as STEAMER have demonstrated the potential of ICAI research and development in training. However, many replications and expansions are needed to confirm the importance of ICAI systems in various training and educational settings.

Accessibility to ICAI systems is a problem which must be quickly overcome by educators and trainers. More ICAI programs need to be developed on emerging high-performance microcomputers which are presently available to educators and trainers. Most present ICAI programming languages and tools are not available to educators or trainers because of their high costs and the limitations of hardware usually available in education and training settings. Educators and trainers will require both access to hardware, tools, and training if they are to participate in the development and evaluation of ICAI programs. The increasing availability of expert systems development tools and AI languages for microcomputers will accelerate research and development of ICAI in education and training. During the next five to ten years, educators and trainers will need to carefully select AI applications which are effective and useful in their classrooms or training centers. We plan to further explore ICAI research efforts so that we can become better developers and consumers. In addition, educators and trainers need the opportunity to use and evaluate ICAI programs to determine the efficacy of their features and usefulness in educational settings. At present, these ICAI programs have not been commercially available. The increasing availabilitiy of sophisticated microcomputers in education and training settings should greatly improve accessibility during the next five years.

In the future, the computer will serve as a multimedia tool. Linkages between computers and other media devices such as videodisc, CD-ROM, optical scanners, and other peripheral devices are crucial to overcoming the limits of the computer in education and training. Obviously, the present levels of sound and graphics on computers in most education and training settings are unacceptable for effective teaching. The linkage of media devices will significantly improve the quality of delivery and interface systems available for computer-based adaptive systems. The graphic and sound strengths of other media must be controlled by the computer program to maximize effective teaching processes and learning environment development both now and in the future. Yet to be seriously considered is the power of joining hypermedia with telecommunication technology, computer networking, and ICAI systems. The education and training possibilities of linking learners around the world to knowledge and information sources are constantly improving. We have difficulty visualizing the effects of students around the world using ICAI systems and engaging in dialogues with other students who are also engaged in the same learning process, but we have no such difficulty in visualizing its bright potential.

The expert systems development processes of planning, design, prototype construction, and evaluation are required in the development of expert and ICAI systems. A production team consisting of AI programmers and cognitive researchers should also include instructional designers, domain experts, and expert teachers and trainers. An emerging methodology for ICAI development is to separately develop each of the components—the simulation, the expertise module, the student module, and the teaching module. Because of the complexity of ICAI systems, all modules are not fully developed in each prototype. Although this modular approach to development is appealing from both a research and development perspective, in the near future a complete ICAI system should be developed and evaluated. The modular structure of ICAI systems lends itself to the team design approach which is perferred, but seldom used, in education and training. The different modules beg for specialized expertise to be applied to them in prototype development and seem likely to yield synergy among components of the final product.

The simulation module provides an exciting opportunity for both motivating learning in education and real-world applications in training. We believe that effectively implemented simulations will significantly impact the motivation of learners of all ages. While learning complex things may involve great effort and truly require hard work, the current and developing technologies, if properly used, leave little reason for instruction to be boring, tedious or passive. The observation of students and trainees engaged in an interesting simulation shows the potential of this module. However, the limited quality and quantity of simulations in education and training settings has not allowed most educators and trainers to observe the real potential of this technology. Equally limiting is the fact that few simulations provide any level of intelligence in teaching or coaching. When students or trainees are confused or fail to acquire prerequisite knowledge, presently available simulations are unable to intervene. Although simulations presently provide opportunities for real-world applications, they also often provide real world frustations without effective monitoring, guidance, or teaching.

Traditionally, the expertise or knowledge module is developed as an expert system prior to the development of the other modules. The use of microcomputer-based expert systems as the expertise module for an ICAI program or an articulate expert system has exciting potential for the development of ICAI. These articulate expert systems can additionally serve as job performance aids to educators and trainers. Prototype expert consultants systems, computerized job aids, and decision support systems are slowly emerging in all areas of education and training. With adaptation, these expert systems can be converted to the expertise module of an ICAI system for effective use in training and education.

The teaching module should become the most important area of ICAI research and development. ICAI must select effective instructional approaches based upon research and best practices related to adaptive teaching and individualized instruction. To be a technology which significantly impacts the roles of educators and trainers, an ICAI system must be designed to incorporate the expertise of the best practitioners as well as the knowledge base from relevant research on teaching. The emphasis on "reactive learning environments" should be replaced with an emphasis on "proactive learning environments." We are strongly biased toward a systematic and direct instruction approach which is not present in ICAI prototypes. We feel that teaching research supports the importance of clear and effective teacher directed instruction. Continuation of the limited discovery learning approaches as the only instructional alternative will definitely lead to the failure of ICAI research to significantly impact education and training. At the present time, ICAI systems have failed to examine the potential impact of an effective teaching module on the successful performance of students or trainees. Research on a range of teaching and learning options is a critical need area for ICAI research and development.

Research on student modeling should continue. Qualitative models of the student should be combined with quantitative models to create an adaptive teaching system. This system should include both relevant microadaptation and macroadaptation of learner variables including cognitive and affective abilities. Although we are interested in the student modules which have been demonstrated in ICAI prototypes, we are deeply concerned about the assumptions that student error and floundering is necessary to effective learning. This assumption requires extensive testing prior to acceptance. For example, precision teaching and direct instruction research indicates that floundering is detrimental to students and trainees who are attempting to memorize facts and information. However, the complex issue of when to clearly teach and prevent errors in skill training such as driver education or equipment usage rather than to encourage floundering has not been determined by present research findings. Obviously, resolving when and how to teach complex problem solving abilities will require extensive research and evaluation efforts.

Spurred by the knowledge that whether instruction is individualized or not, learning always is, educators and trainers have continually yearned for the capability to implement truly individualized and adaptive instruction. The belief is strongly in us that individualized instruction (both micro- and macroadaptation) is required to maximize individualized learning outcomes in efficient fashion. While the characteristics and demands of our daily teaching environments and resource base realistically block many attempts at increasing the extent to which instruction is actually individualized, we recognize that the major blockade we have faced is the absence of a coherent, feasible delivery technology. If we pursue ICAI development and use other AI technologies, then that blockade can be removed. Educators and trainers must come to truly believe that individualized instruction is practical and feasible. And that may be the single greatest contribution the field of AI can make to the fields of education and training for the 21st Century.

TOPICAL REFERENCES

Adaptive Teaching

Corno, L., & Snow, R.E. (1986). Adapting teaching to individual differences among learners. In *Handbook of research on teaching*. M.C. Wittrock (Ed.) New York: Macmillan Publishing Company.

Glaser, R. (1977). *Adaptive education: Individual diversity and learning*. New York: Holt, Rinehart and Winston.

Intelligent Computer-Assisted Instruction

Barr, W., & Clancey, W.J. (Eds.) (1983). *Handbook of artificial intelligence–Vol. III*. Los Altos, CA: William Kaufmann, Inc.

Dede, C. (1986). A review and synthesis of recent research in intelligent computer-assisted instruction. *Journal of Man-Machine Studies*, *24*, 329-353.

Dede, C., & Swigger, K. (1988). The evolution of instructional design principles for intelligent computer-assisted instruction. *Journal of Instructional Development*, *11* (1), 15-22.

AI and ICAI

Kearsley, G. (Ed.) (1987). *Artificial intelligence and instruction— Applications and methods*. Reading, MA: Addison-Wesley Publishing.

Wenger, E. (1987). *Artificial intelligence and tutoring systems— Computational and cognitive approaches to the communication of knowledge*. Los Altos, CA: Morgan Kaufmann Publishers.

CAI and ICAI

Chambers, J.A., & Sprecher, J.W. (1983). *Computer-assisted instruction—Its use in the classroom.* Englewood Cliffs, NJ: Prentice-Hall, Inc.

O'Shea, T., & Self, J. (1983). *Learning and teaching with computers—Artificial intelligence in education* . Englewood Cliffs, NJ: Prentice-Hall, Inc.

Park, O., Perez, R.S., & Seidel, R.J. (1987). Intelligent CAI: Old wine in new bottles, or a new vintage?" In G. Kearsley (Ed.) *Artificial intelligence and instruction—Applications and methods.* Reading, MA: Addison-Wesley Publishing.

Park, O., & Seidel, R.J. (1987). Conventional CBI versus intelligent CAI: Suggestions for the development of future systems. *Educational Technology, 27* (5), 15-21.

Intelligent Tutoring Systems

Sleeman, D., & Brown, J.S. (Eds.) (1982). *Intelligent tutoring systems.* London: Academic Press.

Wenger, E. (1987). *Artificial intelligence and tutoring systems— Computational and cognitive approaches to the communication of knowledge.* Los Altos, CA: Morgan Kaufmann Publishers.

Intelligent Learning Environments

Dede, C. (1987). Empowering Environments, Hypermedia and Microworlds. *The Computing Teacher, 14* (11), 20-24.

Lawler, R.W. (1987). Learning environments: Now, then, and someday. In R.W. Lawler and M. Yazdani (Eds.) *Artificial intelligence and education: Learning environments and intelligent tutoring systems.* Norwood, NJ: Ablex Publishing.

REFERENCES

Ahlers, R.H., Evans, R.A., & O'Neil, H.F., Jr. (1986). Expert systems for Department of Defense training. *Journal of Computer-Based Instruction, 13* (2), 29.

Allen, B.S., & Carter, C.D. (1988). Expert systems and interactive video tutorials: Separating strategies from subject matter. *Journal of Computer-Based Instruction, 15* (4), 123-130.

Anderson, J.R. (1983). *The architecture of cognition.* Cambridge, MA: Harvard University Press.

Anderson, J.R. (1985). *Cognitive psychology and its implications.* San Francisco: W.H. Freeman.

Annarino, A.A. (1983). The teaching-learning process: A systematic instructional strategy. *Journal of Physical Education, Recreation and Dance, 54* (3), 51-53.

Arden, B.W. (Ed.) (1980). *What can be automated.* Cambridge, MA: MIT Press.

Atkinson, R.C. (1972). Ingredients for a theory of instruction. *American Psychologist, 27,* 921-931.

Barr, W., & Feigenbaum, E.A. (Eds.) (1981). *Handbook of artificial intelligence—Vol. I.* Los Altos, CA: William Kaufmann, Inc.

Barr, W., & Feigenbaum, E.A. (Eds.) (1982). *Handbook of artificial intelligence—Vol. II.* Los Altos, CA: William Kaufmann, Inc.

Barr, W., & Clancey, W.J. (1982). Application -oriented AI research: Education. In P.R. Cohen, P & E.A. Feigenbaum (Eds.), *Handbook of artificial intelligence—Vol. II.* Los Altos, CA: William Kaufmann, Inc.

Becker, W.C., & Carnine, D.W. (1980). Direct instruction—An effective approach to educational intervention with the disadvantaged and low performs. *Advances in Clinical Child Psychology, 3,* 430-473.

Bonner, J. (1987). Computer courseware: Frame-based or intelligent? *Educational Technology, 27* (3), 30-32.

Bork, A. (1986). Nontrival, nonintelligent computer-based learning. Technical Report. Educational Technology Center, University of California, Irving, CA.

Brachman, R.J., Armarel, S., Engelman, C., Engelmore, R.S., Feigenbaum, E.A., & Wilkins, D.E. (1983). What are expert systems? In F. Hayes-Roth, D.A.Waterman, & D.B. Lenat, (Eds.) *Building Expert Systems*. Reading, MA: Addison-Wesley Publishing.

Brand, S. (1988). *The Media Lab—Inventing the future at M.I.T.* New York: Penguin Books.

Breuer, K., & Hajovy, H. (1987). Adaptive instructional simulations to improve learning of cognitive strategies. *Educational Technology, 27* (5), 29-32.

Brody, J.E. (1979). Teacher behavior and its effects. *Journal of Educational Psychology, 71,* 733-750.

Brody, J.E., & Good, T.L. (1986). Teacher behavior and student achievement. In M.C. Wittrock (Ed.), *Handbook of Research on Teaching*. New York: Macmillan Publishing.

Brown, J.S., & Burton, R.R. (1974). SOPHIE: A sophisticated instructional environment for teaching electronic troubleshooting. *Final Report*. Cambridge, MA: Bolt, Beranek and Newman.

Brown, J.S., & Burton, R.R. (1978). Diagonostic models for procedural bugs in basic mathematics skills. *Cognitive Science, 2,* 155-191.

Buchanan, B.G., & Shortliffe, E.H. (1984). *Rule-based expert systems—The MYCIN experiments of the Stanford Heuristic Programming Project.* Reading, MA: Addison-Wesley Publishing.

Bunderson, C.V. (1970). The computer and instructional design. In W.H. Holzman (Ed.), *Computer-Assisted Instruction, Testing and Guidance*. New York: Harper and Row.

Bunderson, C.V., & Inouye, D.K. (1987). The evolution of computer-aided educational delivery systems. In R.M. Gagne (Ed.), *Instructional Technology: Foundations*. Hillsdale, NJ: Lawrence Erlbaum Associates Publishers.

Burton, R.R. (1982). Diagnosing bugs in a simple procedural skill. In D.H. Sleeman, and J.S. Brown (Eds.) *Intelligent Tutoring Systems*. London: Academic Press.

Burton, R.R., & Brown, J.S. (1979). An investigation of computer coaching for informal learning activities. *International Journal of Man-Machine Studies, 11,* 5-24.

Carbonell, J.R. (1970a). AI in CAI: An artificial intelligence approach to computer-assisted instruction. *IEEE Transactions on Man-Machine Systems, 11* (4), 190-202.

Carbonell, J.R. (1970b). Mixed-initiative man-computer instructional dialogues. Doctoral Disseration, Massachusetts Institute of Technology, Cambridge, MA.

Carr, B., & Goldstein, I.P. (1977). Overlays: A theory of modeling for computer-aided instruction. AI Lab Memo 406. Cambridge, MA: Massachusetts Institute of Technology.

Carr, C. (1988). Skilling America: The potential of intelligent job aids. *Educational Technology, 28* (4), 22-25.

Carrico, M.A., Girard, J.E., & Jones, J.P. (1989). *Building knowledge systems— Developing and managing rule-based applications.* New York: Intertext–McGraw-Hill.

Cauderhead, J. (1981). A psychological approach to research on teachers' classroom decison making. *British Educational Research Journal, 7,* 51-57.

Chambers, J.A., & Sprecher, J.W. (1983). *Computer-assisted instruction—Its use in the classroom.* Englewood Cliffs, NJ: Prentice-Hall, Inc.

Clancey, W.J. (1986). From GUIDON to NEOMYCIN and HERACLES in twenty short sessons: ORN Final Report 1979-1985. *AI Magazine,* 7(3), 40-60.

Clancey, W.J. (1987). *Knowledge-based tutoring—The GUIDON program.* Cambridge, MA: The MIT Press.

Clancey, W.J., & Shortliffe, E.H. (Eds.) (1984). *Readings in medical artificial intelligence: The first decade.* Reading, MA: Addison-Wesley Publishing Company.

Clark, C.M., & Peterson, P.L. (1986). Teachers' thought processes. In *Handbook of research on teaching* (Ed.) M.C. Wittrock. New York: Macmillan Publishing.

Clocksin, W.F., & Mellish, C.S. (1984). *Programming in Prolog.* New York: Springer-Verlag.

Coale, K. (1989). The Body Electric. *MacUser, 5* (3), 100-104.

Cohen, P.R., & Feignenbaum, E.A. (Eds.) (1982). *Handbook of artificial intelligence—Vol. III.* Los Altos, CA: William Kaufmann, Inc.

Colbourn, M., & McLeod, J. (1983). Computer guided educational diagnosis: A prototype expert system. *Journal of Special Education Technology, 6* (1), 30-39.

Conger, J.J. (1957). The meaning and measurement of intelligence. *Rocky Mountain Medical Journal,* June.

Corno, L., & Snow, R.E. (1986). Adapting teaching to individual differences among learners. In M.C. Wittrock (Ed.), *Handbook of research on teaching.* New York: Macmillan Publishing Company.

Costanzo, W.V. (1989). *The electronic text: Learning to write, read, and reason with computers.* Englewood Cliffs, NJ: Educational Technology Publications.

Crowder, N.A. (1962). Intrinsic and extrinsic programming. In J.E. Coulson (Ed.), *Proceedings of the Conference on Applications of Digital Computers to Automated Instruction.* New York: Wiley.

Daynes, R., & Butler, B. (1984). *The videodisc book.* Somerset, NJ: John Wiley & Son.

Dear, B.L. (1986). Artificial intelligence techniques: Applications for courseware development. *Educational Technology, 26* (7), 7-15.

DeBloois, M.L. (1982). *Videodisc/microcomputer courseware design.* Englewood Cliffs, NJ: Educational Technology Publications.

DeBloois, M.L. (1985). *Effectiveness of interactive videodisc training.* Salt Lake City, UT: Learning Link Corporation.

Dede, C. (1983). The likely evolution of computer use in schools. *Educational Leadership, 41* (1), 22-24.

Dede, C. (1986). A review and synthesis of recent research in intelligent computer-assisted instruction. *Journal of Man-Machine Studies , 24,* 329-353.

Dede, C. (1987). Empowering environments, hypermedia and microworlds. *The Computing Teacher, 14* (11), 20-24.

Dede, C. (1989). Planning guidelines for emerging instructional technologies. *Educational Technology, 29* (4), 7-12.

Dede, C., & Swigger, K. (1988). The evolution of instructional design principles for intelligent computer-assisted instruction. *Journal of Instructional Development, 11* (1), 15-22.

DeGroot, A.D. (1965). *Thought and choice in chess.* New York: Basic Books Inc.

Dreyfus, H.L., & Dreyfus, S.E. (1986). *Mind over machine.* New York: The Free Press.

Duchastel, P. (1986). *ICAI systems: Issues in computer tutoring.* Technical Report, Department of Educational Technology, University of Laval, Quebec.

Engelmann, S., & Carnine, D. (1982). *Theory of instruction: Principles and applications.* New York: Irvington Publishers, Inc.

Feigenbaum, E.A. (1978). The art of artificial intelligence: Themes and case studies of knowledge engineering. In *AFIPS Conference Proceedings of the 1978 National Computer Conference*, Vol. 47 (Anaheim, CA), 227-240.

Feigenbaum, E.A., & McCorduck, P. (1983). *The fifth generation—Artificial intelligence and Japan's challenge to the world.* Reading, MA: Addison-Wesley Publishing.

Ferrara, J.M., Prater, M.A., & Baer, R. (1987). Using an expert system for complex conceptual training. *Educational Technology, 27* (5), 43-46.

Fischler, M.A., & Firschein, O. (1987). *Intelligence: The eye, the brain, and the computer.* Reading, MA: Addison-Wesley Publishing.

Fogarty, J.L., Wang, M.C., & Creek, R. (1982). A descriptive study of experienced and novice teachers' interactive instructional decision processes. Paper presented at annual meeting of the American Educational Research Association, New York City.

Gable, A., & Page, C.V. (1980). The use of artificial intelligence technique in computer-assisted instruction: An overview. In D.F. Walker & R.D. Hess (Eds.) *Instructional Software.* Belmont, CA: Wadsworth, 257-268.

Gagne, R.M. (1985). *The conditions of learning and theory of instruction.* New York: Holt, Rinehart and Winston.

Gardner, H. (1985). *The mind's new science .* New York: Basic Books.

Gayeski, D.M. (1989). Why information technologies fail. *Educational Technology, 24* (2), 9-17.

Gevarter, W.B. (1985). *Intelligent machines—An introductory perspective of artificial intelligence and robotics.* Englewood Cliffs, NJ: Prentice-Hall, Inc.

Glaser, R. (1977). *Adaptive education: Individual diversity and learning.* New York: Holt, Rinehart and Winston.

Goldstein, I.P., & Papert, S. (1977). Artificial intelligence, language, and the study of knowledge. *Cognitive Science, 1* (1), 1-21.

Gooler, D. (1989). Preparing teachers to use technologies: Can universities meet the challenge? *Educational Technology, 24* (3), 22-25.

Greeno, J.G. (1986). Advancing cognitive science through development of Advanced instructional systems. *Machine-Mediated Learning, 1* (4), 327-343.

Hajovy, H., & Christensen, D.L. (1987). Intelligent computer-assisted instruction: The next generation. *Educational Technology, 27* (5), 9-14.

Harmon, P. (1984). Performance engineering as an expert system. *Performance & Instruction Journal, 23* (9), 4-6.

Harmon, P. (1986). Expert systems, job aids, and the future of instructional technology. *Performance & Instruction Journal, 25* (2), 26-28.

Harmon, P., & King, D. (1985). *Expert systems—Artificial intelligence in business.* New York: John Wiley & Sons.

Harmon, P., Maus, R., & Morrissey, W. (1988). *Expert systems tools and applications.* New York: John Wiley & Sons.

Harris, L.R., & Davis, D.B. (1986). *Artificial intelligence enters the marketplace.* Toronto: Bantam Books.

Hayes-Roth, F., Waterman, D.A., & Lenat, D.B. (1983). *Building expert systems.* Reading, MA: Addison-Wesley Publishing.

Hayes-Roth, F. (1985). Rule-based systems. *Communication of the ACM, 28* (9), 921-932.

Haynes, J.A., Pilato, V.H., & Malouf, D.B. (1987). Expert systems for educational decision-making. *Educational Technology, 27* (5), 37-42.

Heinich, R., Molenda, M., & Russell, J.D. (1989). *Instructional media and the new technologies of instruction.* New York: John Wiley & Son.

Hofmeister, A.M. (1984). *Microcomputer applications in the classroom.* New York: Holt, Rinehart and Winston.

Hofmeister, A.M. (1986). Formative evaluation in the development and validation of expert systems in education. *Computational Intelligence, 2* (2), 65-67.

Hofmeister, A.M., & Ferrara, J.M. (1986). Expert systems and special education. *Exceptional Children, 53,* 235-239.

Hofmeister A.M., & Lubke, M.M. (1986). Expert systems: Implications for the diagnosis and treatment of learning disabilities. *Learning Disability Quarterly, 9,* 133-137.

Hollan, J.D., Hutchens, E.L., & Weitzman, L.M. (1987). STEAMER: An interactive inspectable simulation-based training system. *AI Magazine, 5* (2), 15-27.

Hopper, G.M., & Mandell, S.L. (1984). *Understanding computers*. St. Paul, MN: West Publishing.

Hunt, E., Lunneborg, C., & Lewis, J. (1975). What does it mean to be high verbal? *Cognitive Psychology.*

Iuppa, N.V. (1984). *A practical guide to interactive video design.* White Plains, NY: Knowledge Industry Publications.

Johnson, G. (1986). *Machinery of the mind—Inside the new science of artificial intelligence.* Redmond, WA: Microsoft Press.

Johnson, W.L., & Soloway, E. (1985). PROUST. *Byte, 10,* 4.

Jonassen, D.H. (1989). *Hypertext/Hypermedia.* Englewood Cliffs, NJ: Educational Technology Publications.

Jones, M.K. (1989). *Human-computer interaction: A design guide.* Englewood Cliffs, NJ: Educational Technology Publications.

Juell, P., & Wasson, J. (1988). A comparison of input and output for a knowledge based system for educational diagnosis. *Educational Technology, 28* (3), 19-23.

Kaufman, R. (1982). Means and ends—Needs assessment, needs analysis, and front-end analysis. *Educational Technology, 22* (11), 33-34.

Kaufman, R. (1983). A holistic planning model. *Performance & Instruction Journal, 22* (8), 3-15.

Kearsley, G. (Ed.) (1987). *Artificial intelligence and instruction—Applications and methods.* Reading, MA: Addison-Wesley Publishing.

Kearsley, G. (1988). Validation of an expert system: The CBT analyst. *Journal of Computer-Based Instruction, 15* (2), 61-64.

Kinnucan, P. (1984). Computers that think like experts. *High Technology,* January, 30-42.

Knezek, G.A. (1988). Intelligent tutoring systems and ICAI. *The Computing Teacher, 15* (6), 11-13.

Knirk, F.G., & Gustafson, K.L. (1986). *Instructional technology—A systematic approach to education.* New York: Holt, Rinehart and Winston.

Lawler, R.W. (1987). Learning environments: Now, then, and someday. In R.W. Lawler and M. Yazdani (Eds.) *Artificial intelligence and education: Learning environments and intelligent tutoring systems.* Norwood, NJ: Ablex Publishing.

Lawler, R.W., & Yazdani, M. (Eds.) (1987). *Artificial intelligence and education: Learning environments and intelligent tutoring systems.* Norwood, NJ: Ablex Publishing.

Lippert, R. (1988). Refinement of students' knowledge during the development of expert systems. Unpublished Doctoral Dissertation, University of Minnesota, Minneapolis, MN.

Lippert, R. (1989). Expert systems: Tutors, tools, and tutees. *Journal of Computer-Based Instruction, 16* (1), 11-19.

Lubke, M. (1987). The development and validation of an expert system based effective teaching inservice in remedial mathematics instruction. Unpublished Doctoral Disseration. Utah State University, Logan, UT.

Mandl, H., & Lesgold, A. (1988). *Learning issues for intelligent tutoring systems.* New York: Springer-Verlag.

Martindale, E.S. (1987). An expert system to train secondary special education teachers in language arts instruction. Unpublished Doctoral Dissertation, Utah State University, Logan, UT.

Martindale, E.S., & Hofmeister, A.M. (1988). An expert system for on-site instructional advice. *Educational Technology, 28* (7), 18-20.

McCarthy, J. (1978). History of LISP. *SIGPLAN Notices, 14*, 217-223.

McFarland, T.D., McFarland, M.R., Ragan, S.R., & Kottkey, D. (1987). A expert system based simulation for nurse training. Presentation at Annual Conference of Association for the Development of Computer-Based Instructional Systems. Oakland, CA.

Merrill, M.D. (1987). An expert system for instructional design. *IEEE Expert.* Summer, 32-40.

Merrill, M.D. (1988). The role of tutorial and experiential models of intelligent tutoring systems. *Educational Technology, 28* (7), 7-18.

Merrill, M.D. (1988). Software and theory. *Educational Technology, 28* (10), 59.

Merrill, M.D., & Tennyson, R.D. (1977). *Teaching concepts: An instructional design guide.* Englewood Cliffs, NJ: Educational Technology Publications.

Michaelsen, R.H., Michie, D, & Boulanger, A. (1985). The technology of expert systems. *BYTE Magazine*, April.

Miller, D.C. (1987). CD ROM joins the new media homesteaders. *Educational Technology, 27* (3), 33.

Minsky, M. (1985). *The society of mind.* New York: Simon and Schuster.

Mishkoff, H.C. (1985). *Understanding artificial intelligence.* Dallas, TX: Texas Instrument.

Nelson, T.H. (1988). The call of the ocean: Hypertext universal and open. *HyperAge—The Journal of HyperThinking,* May-June, 5-7.

Nelson, W.A., Magliaro, S., & Sherman, T.M. (1988). The intellectual content of instructional design. *Journal of Instructional Development, 11* (1), 29-35.

Newell, A., & Simon, H.A. (1972). *Human problem solving.* Englewood Cliffs, NJ: Prentice-Hall.

Nilsson, N.J. (1980). *Principles of artificial intelligence.* Palo Alto, CA: Tioga.

Ohlsson, S. (1987). Some principles of intelligent tutoring. In R. Lawler and M. Yazdani (Eds.) *Artificial intelligence and education: Learning environments and intelligent tutoring systems.* Norwood, NJ: Ablex Publishing.

O'Neil, H.F., Anderson, C.L., & Freeman, J.A. (1986). Research on teaching in the Armed Forces. In M.C. Wittrock (Ed.) *Handbook of research on teaching* . New York: Macmillan Publishing.

O'Shea, T. (1979). *Self-improving teaching systems: An application of artificial intelligence to computer-aided instruction.* Basel: Birkhaser Verlag.

O'Shea, T., & Self, J. (1983). *Learning and teaching with computers—Artificial intelligence in education* . Englewood Cliffs, NJ: Prentice-Hall, Inc.

Papert, S. (1980). *Mindstorms: Children, computers, and powerful ideas.* New York: Basic Books, Inc.

Park, O. (1988). Functional characteristics of intelligent computer-assisted instruction: Intelligent features. *Educational Technology, 28* (6), 7-14.

Park, O., Perez, R.S., & Seidel, R.J. (1987). Intelligent CAI: Old wine in new bottles, or a new vintage? In G. Kearsley, (Ed.) *Artificial intelligence and instruction—Applications and methods.* Reading, MA: Addison-Wesley Publishing.

Park, O., & Seidel, R.J. (1987). Conventional CBI versus intelligent CAI: suggestions for the development of future systems. *Educational Technology, 27* (5), 15-21.

Parry, J.D. (1986). The development and validation of an expert system for reviewing a special education practice. Unpublished Doctoral Dissertation, Utah State University, Logan, UT.

Parry, J.D., & Hofmeister, A.M. (1986). Development and validation of an expert system for special educators. *Learning Disabilitiy Quarterly, 9* (1), 44-48.

Pearl, J. (1984). *Heuristics: Intelligent strategies for computer problem solving.* Reading, MA: Addison-Wesley Publishing.

Peat, D. (1985). *Artificial intelligence: How machines think.* New York: Baen Books.

Poirot, J.L., & Norris, C.A. (1988). AI programming languages. *The Computing Teacher, 15* (1), 17-19.

Pollock, J., & Grabinger, R.S. (1989). Expert systems: Instructional design potential. *Educational Technology, 29* (4), 35-39.

Prater, M.A. (1986). Expert systems technology and concept instruction: Training educators to accurately classify learning disabled students. Unpublished Doctoral Dissertation, Utah State University, Logan, UT.

Pylyshyn, Z.W. (1979). Validating computational models: A critique of Anderson's indeterminacy of representation claim. *Psychological Review, 86* (4), 383-394.

Pylyshyn, Z.W. (1984). *Computation and cognition: Toward a foundation for cognitive science.* Cambridge, MA: MIT Press.

Pylyshyn, Z. (1987). Cognitive science. In S.C. Shapiro (Ed.) *The encyclopedia of artificial intelligence.* New York: John Wiley & Sons.

Ragan, S. & McFarland, T.D. (1987). Applications of expert systems in education: A technology for decision-makers. *Educational Technology*, *27* (5), 33-36.

Rauch-Hindin, W.B. (1988). *A guide to commercial artificial intelligence.* Englewood Cliffs, NJ: Prentice Hall.

Reigeluth, C.M., & Schwartz, E. (1989). An instructional theory for the design of computer-based simulations. *Journal of Computer-Based Instruction, 16* (1), 1-10.

Reynolds, M.C., & Birch, J.W. (1988). *Adaptive mainstreaming—A primer for teachers and principals.* New York: Longman.

Richer, M.H., & Clancey, W.J. (1985). GUIDON-WATCH: A graphic interface for viewing a knowledge-based system, *IEEE Computer Graphics and Applications, 5* (11), 51-64.

Roberts, F.C., & Park, O. (1983). Intelligent computer-assisted instruction: An explanation and overview. *Educational Technology, 23* (12), 7-11.

Rodriguez, S.R. (1988). Needs assessment and analysis: Tools for change. *Educational Technology, 28* (1), 23-28.

Romiszowski, A.J. (1986). *Developing auto-instructional materials—From programmed texts to CAL and interactive video.* London: Kogan Page.

Romiszowski, A.J. (1987). Expert systems in education and training: Automated job aids or sophisticated instructional media. *Educational Technology, 27* (10), 22-30.

Rosenberg, R. (1987). A critical analysis of research on intelligent tutoring systems. *Educational Technology, 27* (11), 7-13.

Rubinstein, M.F. (1975). *Patterns of problem solving.* Englewood Cliffs, NJ: Prentice- Hall.

Schank, R.C. (1984). *The cognitive computer—On language, learning, and artificial intelligence.* Reading, MA: Addison-Wesley Publishing.

Schwartz, E. (1987). *The educator's handbook to interactive videodisc.* Washington, DC: Assocation for Educational Communication and Technology.

Scriven, M. (1967). The methodology of evaluation. *Perspectives of curriculum evaluation. AERA Monograph Series,* Rand McNally, Chicago, IL. 39-83.

Sculley, J. (1987). *Odyssey.* New York: Harper & Row.

Sculley, J. (1989). The Knowledge Navigator. *PC AI, 3* (1), 31.

Shafer, D. (1986). *Artificial intelligence programming on the Macintosh.* Indianapolis, IN: Howard W. Sams & Co.

Shapiro, S.C. (Ed.) (1987). *Encyclopedia of Artificial Intelligence—Vol. I & II.* New York: John Wiley & Sons.

Shelly, G.B. and Cashman, T.J. (1984). *Computer fundamentals for an information age .* Brea, CA: Anaheim Publishing.

Simon, H.A. (1969). *Science of the artificial.* Cambridge, MA: MIT Press.

Simon, H.A. (1973). The structure of ill-structured problems. *Artificial Intelligence, 4,* 181-201.

Simon, H.A. (1981). Studying human intelligence by creating artificial intelligence. *American Scientist, 69* (3), 177-181.

Simon, H.A. (1987). Guest foreword. In S.C. Shapiro (Ed.) *Encyclopedia of artificial intelligence—Vol. I.* NewYork: John Wiley & Sons.

Sleeman, D.H. (1982). Assessing aspects of competence in basic algebra. In D.H. Sleeman & J.S. Brown (Eds.) *Intelligent tutoring systems.* London: Academic Press.

Sleeman, D. & Brown, J.S. (Eds.) (1982). *Intelligent tutoring systems.* London: Academic Press.

Sokolowski, R. (1988). Natural and artificial intelligence. In S.R. Graubard (Ed.) *The artificial intelligence debate—False starts, real foundations.* Cambridge, MA: MIT Press.

Starfield, A.M., Butala, K.L.., England, M.M., & Smith, K.A. (1983). Mastering engineering concepts by building an expert system. *Engineering Education,* November, 104-107.

Sternberg, R.J. (1982). *Handbook of human intelligence* . Cambridge: Cambridge University Press.

Stevens, A.L., & Collins, A. (1977). The goal structure of a socratic tutor. BNN Report, Cambridge, MA: Bolt Beranek and Newman, Inc.

Suppes, P. (1979). Observations about the applications of artificial intelligence research to education. In D.F. Walker & R.D. Hess (Eds.), *Instructional Software.* Belmont, CA: Wadsworth, 298-308.

Suppes, P. (Ed.) (1981). *University-level computer assisted instruction at Stanford: 1968-1980.* Stanford, CA: Institute for Mathematical Studies in the Social Science.

Teknowledge, Inc. (1985). M.1 reference manual. Palo Alto, CA: Teknowledge, Inc.

Tennyson, R.D. (1980). Instructional control strategies and content structure as design variables in concept acquisition using computer-based instruction. *Journal of Educational Psychology, 72* (4), 525-532.

Tennyson, R.D. (1987). MAIS: An education alternative of ICAI. *Educational Technology, 27* (5), 22-28.

Tennyson, R.D., Christiansen, D.L., & Park, O. (1984). The Minnesota Adaptive Instructional System: An intelligent CBI system. *Journal of Computer-Based Instruction, 11* (1), 2-13.

Tennyson, R.D., & Cocchiarella, M.J. (1987). An empirically based instructional design theory for teaching concepts. *Review of Educational Research, 56* (1), 40-71.

Tennyson, R.D., & Ferrara, J. (1987). Introduction to special issue: Artificial intelligence in education. *Educational Technology, 27* (5), 7-8.

Tennyson, R.D., & Park, O. (1984). Computer-based adaptive instructional systems: A review of empirically based models. *Machine-Mediated Learning, 1* (2), 129-153.

Tennyson, R.D., & Rothen, W. (1979). Management of computer-based instruction: Design of an adaptive control strategy. *Journal of Computer-Based Instruction, 5* (3), 63-71.

Tiemann, P.W., & Markle, S.M. (1984). On getting expertise into an expert system. *Performance & Instruction Journal, 23* (11), 25-29.

Touretzky, D.S. (1984). *LISP—A gentle introduction to symbolic computation.* New York: Harper & Row, Publishers.

Trollip, S.R., & Lippert, R.C. (1987). Constructing knowledge bases: A promising instructional tool. *Journal of Computer-Based Instruction, 14* (2), 44-48.

Turing, A.M. (1963). Computing machinery and intelligence. In E.A. Feigenbaum and J. Feldman (Eds.) *Computers and Thought.* New York: MeGraw-Hill. Original work published 1950.

Turkle, S. (1984). *The scecond self: Computers and the human spirit.* New York: Simon and Schuster.

Von Neumann, J. (1958). *The computer and the brain.* New Haven, CN: Yale University Press.

Waltz, D.I. (1975). Generating schematic descriptions from drawings of scenes with shadows. In P.H. Winston (Ed.), *The psychology of computer vision.* New York: McGraw-Hill.

Waterman, DA. (1986). *A guide to expert systems.* Reading, MA: Addison-Wesley Publishing.

Wedman, J.F. (1987). Citation patterns in the computer-based instruction literature. *Journal of Computer-Based Instruction, 14* (3), 91-95.

Weiss, S.M. (1984). *A practical guide to designing expert systems.* Totowa, NJ: Rowman & Allanheld.

Weizenbaum, J. (1976). *Computer power and human reason.* San Francisco, CA: W.H. Freeman.

Wenger, E. (1987). *Artificial intelligence and tutoring systems—Computational and cognitive approaches to the communication of knowledge.* Los Altos, CA: Morgan Kaufmann Publishers.

Wideman, H.H., & Owston, R.D. (1988). Student development of an expert system: A case study. *Journal of Computer-Based Instruction., 15* (3), 88-94.

Williams, M., Hollan, J., & Stevens, A. (1983.) Human reasoning about a simple physical system. In D. Genter & A. Stevens (Eds.), *Mental Models.* Hillsdale, NJ: Erlbaum.

Winograd, T. (1972). *Understanding natural language.* New York: Academic Press.

Winograd, T. & Flores, F. (1987). *Understanding computers and cognition—A new foundation.* Reading, MA: Addison-Wesley Publishing.

Winston, P.H. (1984). *Artificial intelligence.* Reading, MA: Addison-Wesley Publishing.

Winston, T., & Brady, F. (1987). *Understanding computers and cognition.* Reading, MA: Addison-Wesley Publishing.

Wittrock, M.C. (Ed.) (1986). *The handbook of research in teaching.* New York: Macmillan, Inc.

Woodward, J., & Carnine, D. (1987). Intelligent computer-assisted instruction— A critique. *ADI News, 6* (2), 8-12.

Woolf, B. (1987). Theoretical frontiers in building a machine tutor. In Kearsley, G. (Ed.) *Artificial intelligence and instruction—Applications and methods.* Reading, MA: Addison-Wesley Publishing.

Woolf, B., Blegen, D., Verloop, A., & Jansen, J. (1986). Tutoring the complex industrial process. Proceedings on Artificial Intelligence (AAAI-86). Philadelphia, PA

Yang, J. (1987). Individualized instruction through intelligent computer-assisted Instruction: A perspective. *Educational Technology, 27* (3), 7-15.

AUTHOR INDEX

A

Ahlers, R.H., 228
Allen, B.S., 56, 139, 186, 205, 228
Anderson, C.L., 187, 237
Anderson, J.R., 49, 61, 62, 65, 85, 196, 228
Annarino, A.A., 53, 228
Arden, B.W., 51, 228
Armarel, S., 228
Atkinson, R.C., 188, 228

B

Baer, R., 107, 144, 232
Barr, W., 24, 54, 58, 59, 60, 63, 64, 65, 68, 116, 137, 140, 162, 228
Becker, W., 213, 228
Birch, H.W., 135, 238
Blegen, D., 209, 242
Bonner, J., 193, 228
Bork, A., 228
Boulanger, A., 24, 236
Brachman, R.J., 228
Brady, F., 7, 18, 242
Brand, S., 203, 229
Brody, J.E., 90, 212, 229
Brown, J.S., 28, 184, 196, 198, 212, 215, 229, 240
Buchanan, B.G., 26, 27, 94, 11, 142, 229
Bunderson, C.V., 5, 181, 229
Burton, R.R., 196, 198, 215, 229
Butala, K.L., 119, 240
Butler, B., 205, 231

C

Carbonell, J.R., 188, 196, 230
Carnine, D., 107, 193, 213, 228, 232, 242
Carr, B., 215, 230
Carr, C., 196, 230
Carter, C.D., 56, 139, 186, 205
Cauderhead, J. 90, 230
Chambers, J.A., 230
Christensen, D.L., 182, 184, 187, 190, 233, 240
Clancey, W.J., 15, 30, 31, 50, 94, 161, 177, 178, 189, 193, 196, 211, 212, 213, 215, 228, 230, 238
Clark, C.M., 230
Clocksin, W.F., 117, 230
Coale, K., 69, 230
Cocchiarella, M.J., 241
Cohen, P.R., 23, 67, 230
Colbourn, M., 231
Conger, J.J., 5, 230
Collins, A., 196, 240
Corno, L., 180, 181, 182, 183, 231
Costanzo, W.V., 231
Creek, R., 90, 232
Crowder, N.A., 188, 231

D

Davis, D.B., 157, 233
Daynes, R., 205, 231
Dear, B.L., 231
DeBloois, M.L., 205, 231
Dede, C., 9, 28, 179, 182, 200, 206, 210, 213, 231

Expert Systems in Education and Training

SUBJECT INDEX

A

Adaptive teaching
  computer-based, 183-184
  defined, 179
  described, 179-182
  directions, 219
  future, 177-178
  topical references, 226
Algorithmic, 9
Analogical reasoning, 55
Articulate expert systems, 155-156
  topical references, 173
Artificial intelligence
  defined, 9, 11-12, 32, 40
  directions, 36-38, 73-74
  history, 10
  relationships, 13
  scientists, 18-19
  topical references, 129
AI languages, 115-117
  topical references, 129
AI tools, 108, 114-118
  directions, 120, 125
  topical references, 129
AI hardware, 114-115
  directions, 125

B

Blackboard, 159
BUGGY, 198

C

Cases, 103-107
CLASS.LD, 144
Communication, 109
Computational vision, 22
Construct prototype, 108-110
Cognitive psychology, 16
Cognitive science, 13-15, 32, 40
Compact disc-read only memory
  (CD-ROM), 204
Computer-based adaptive instructional
  systems, 183-184
Computer coaches, 197, 199
Computer science, 17-18, 32, 40
Consistency enforcer, 158-159
Consulting
  computer-based, 137, 140
  defined, 135, 140
  directions, 167
  future, 133-134
  human, 136, 140
  types, 133
  written, 136-137
  topical references, 172
Control structure, 110, 158-159, 164

D

Database, 156-157
DEBUGGY, 198
decision support systems (DSS)
  described, 149, 164, 168
  topical references, 173

249